YALE SOUTHEAST ASIA STUDIES MONOGRAPH SERIES

*Compiled by Dith Pran*

*Introduction by Ben Kiernan*

*Edited by Kim DePaul*

Yale University Press

New Haven and London

MEMOIRS BY SURVIVORS

# Children of

# Cambodia's

# Killing Fields

R

Published with assistance from the
Charles A. Coffin Fund.

An earlier version of "When the Owl
Cries," by Chanrithy Him, appeared
in *Treasures 3: Stories & Art by Students
in Japan & Oregon*, edited by Chris
Weber and published by the Oregon
Students Writing & Art Foundation,
copyright © 1994. Reprinted by
permission.

An earlier version of "My Sadness,"
by Darith Keo, appeared in the
*Modesto Bee*, Modesto, Calif.,
copyright © 1992. Reprinted by
permission.

Designed by James J. Johnson and
set in Nofret Roman type by The
Marathon Group, Durham, North
Carolina. Printed in the United
States of America by Vail-Ballou
Press, Binghamton, New York.

*Library of Congress Cataloging-in-
Publication Data*

Children of Cambodia's killing fields :
memoirs by survivors / compiled by
Dith Pran ; introduction by Ben
Kiernan : edited by Kim DePaul.
    p.  cm. – (Yale Southeast Asia
studies monograph series)
ISBN 0-300-06839-5 (alk. paper)

1. Cambodia–History–1975–
2. Political atrocities–Cambodia.
3. Children–Cambodia–Biography.
I. Dith Pran, 1942–  .  II. Depaul,
Kim.  III. Series : Monograph series
(Yale University. Southeast Asia
Studies)
DS554.8.C46  1997
959.604'2–dc21              96–49804

A catalogue record for this book is
available from the British Library.

The paper in this book meets the
guidelines for permanence and
durability of the Committee on
Production Guidelines for Book
Longevity of the Council on Library
Resources.

10  9  8  7  6  5  4  3  2

*We dedicate this book to all our family members and countrymen
who died in senseless wars and in the
killing fields.*

*A special tribute goes to Dr. Haing S. Ngor,
who carried Dith Pran's message through his portrayal of Pran's life.
He became a co-messenger and fought for justice.*

*We will never forget the Khmer Rouge killing fields.*

# Contents

❀ ❀ ❀

❀
vii

# CONTENTS

# ❀ ❀ ❀
# Compiler's Note

### DITH PRAN

I come from Cambodia, a country that at one time was peaceful and nonaligned. In the mid–1950s, the monarch, Prince Sihanouk, prided himself on the fact that Cambodia was no longer colonized by the French and was neutral. This happiness was short–lived because Cambodia was dragged into the Vietnam War in the 1960s.

The North Vietnamese army extended the Ho Chi Minh Trail to include areas along the border inside Cambodia. The United States under the Nixon administration bombed this North Vietnamese sanctuary and supply route, killing many Cambodian civilians and pushing the Communists deeper and deeper into Cambodia.

Eventually the North Vietnamese army trained a Communist guerrilla group called the Khmer Rouge. The North Vietnamese equipped the Khmer Rouge with Chinese and Soviet weaponry, and the Khmer Rouge became a strong force in the countryside. Except in the north and east, the Cambodian government ruled the cities. In the nearby countryside, the Khmer Rouge kept gaining territory. In the evening, after the government forces went back to their barracks, the Khmer Rouge moved in around the perimeter of the cities. The Khmer Rouge, who claimed to be patriotic, exploited the corruption of the current Lon Nol government and the American bombing. They took towns captive, burned villages, and recruited Khmer youths to join their cause.

Eventually the Khmer Rouge surrounded Phnom Penh, and on April 17, 1975, after five years of civil war, they took control, waving their flag in the streets. Until January 1979 they forced all Cambodians to live in labor camps and work fourteen-to-eighteen-hour days. They fed us one daily bowl of watery rice; they separated families; they destroyed all Cambodian institutions and culture; they systematically tortured and killed innocent people. It is estimated that during this time nearly a third of the Cambodian population was killed due to disease, starvation, or execution.

It is important for me that the new generation of Cambodians and Cambodian Americans become active and tell the world what happened to them and their families under the Khmer Rouge. I want them never to forget the faces of their relatives and friends who were killed during that time. The dead are crying out for justice. Their voices must be heard. It is the responsibility of the survivors to speak out for those who are unable to speak, in order that the genocide and holocaust will never happen again in this world.

The ghosts of the innocent will be on my mind forever. This is why I have compiled these stories. I want future generations to learn about what these survivors, these heroes have gone through and be moved enough to do their part in helping to make the world a better place.

Although you may have seen part of my story in the movie *The Killing Fields*, I hope that in this collection of stories you will come to a greater understanding of the human tragedy the Khmer Rouge have created for the people and country of Cambodia. I hope you will be able to see through the eyes of these Cambodian survivors, who lost their childhood one sunny day in April 1975.

❀ ❀ ❀

# Introduction
## A World Turned Upside Down

**BEN KIERNAN**

$A$lso Georgiana Wife of the Above," said young Pip in Charles Dickens' *Great Expectations*, reading from his father's tombstone. He knew his parents only from their gravesite. *"Also Georgiana.* That's my mother," he explained to the convict Magwitch. Asked about his father, Pip replied, "Him too; late of this parish." Then, to Pip's astonishment, the convict grabbed him and turned him upside down, then back again, until "the church came to itself—for he was so sudden and strong that he made it go head over heels before me, and I saw the steeple under my feet." Once again, he "gave me the most tremendous dip and roll, so that the church jumped over its own weather-cock."[1]

*Children of Cambodia's Killing Fields* provides a child's-eye view of a different, harsher world, one in which Cambodia's children were turned upside down. From 1975 to 1979 the Khmer Rouge regime not only upended the entire Buddhist religion but also mounted history's fiercest ever attack on family life. In the prerevolutionary Khmer language, the word *kruosaa* meant family. But under the Khmer Rouge it came to mean spouse. As the Khmer Rouge redefined the family, they simply excluded children. Now children belonged not to their parents but to Angkar, the Khmer Rouge's ruling organization. Like Pip, Cambodian children were orphaned, deprived of real knowledge of their natural parents, and constantly told how lucky they were to be adopted by their new family.

Almost all Cambodian families were broken up. Yet while Angka suppressed family life, Cambodia became a family dictatorship. Its rulers now consisted of the families of Prime Minister Pol Pot and his brother–in–law, Deputy Prime Minister Ieng Sary (they had married the Khieu sisters). The family network of Mok, Angka's military chief of staff–including his siblings, children, and in–laws–ruled the regime's Southwest Zone heartland and, increasingly, other parts of the country as well.

Most families in Cambodia saw their children taken away and sent to live in barracks or at distant worksites. Especially in the Southwest Zone, people were placed into new social categories on the basis of the recent geographical origin or the assumed political inclinations of their relatives. But this did not mean that extended or even nuclear families could live together, since family "influence"–pernicious word for love–threatened the regime.

As early as 1972, three years before their victory over the Lon Nol regime, the Khmer Rouge in the southwest cast their family ideology into songs that they taught the people living under their control. One, about Khmer Rouge soldiers, went as follows:

> You depend on your grandparents,
> But they are far away.
> You depend on your mother,
> But your mother is at home.
> You depend on your elder sister,
> But she has married a [Lon Nol] soldier . . .
> You depend on the rich people,
> But the rich people oppress the poor people.[2]

The last two lines reveal that the Khmer Rouge placed family relationships in the same category as class relationships. All were portrayed as unreliable if not antagonistic, entanglements to be severed.

In 1977, Khmer Rouge cadres from the Southwest Zone took over much of the rest of the country on behalf of Pol Pot's central leadership. In the eastern part of the country, according to a local peasant, "the new cadres told us to forget about 'familyism' [*kruosaa niyum*] and not to miss our wives and children, whom we were now allowed to visit for only three days every three months."[3] "Familyism," the Khmer Rouge term for missing one's loved ones, became a crime. It was often punishable by death.

Another song, taught by the Khmer Rouge of the Southwest in 1977, vowed "We Children Love Angka Boundlessly."

> Before the revolution, children were poor and lived lives of
>     misery.
> Living like animals, suffering as orphans . . .
> Now the glorious revolution supports us all
> Secure in health, full of strength to develop collective lives.
> With clothes to wear, not cold at night.[4]

Readers may judge the accuracy of these lyrics by reading the rest of this book.

In 1978 a new song, entitled "Children of the Southwest," revealed the role of children in the eyes of the Pol Pot regime:

> We children welcome and greet the armed forces
> who have been vigilant, friends, vigilant in smashing the
>     enemy.
> Heroic combatants and glorious people,
> smashing the imperialists, friends, defeating their lackeys.
> Hurrah, hurrah, we applaud and cheer.
> Bring victory to the armed forces who have been vigilant,
>     friends, smashed the enemy and triumphed.[5]

Readers may judge the accuracy of *these* words by the regime's defeat within a year.

After 1975, with the mass kidnapping of a nation, Angka's prison staff and security forces grew exponentially. When Angka recruited officers to the Santebal, its secret police, the applicants completed an eleven-page biographical form. Most of this form was taken up by no fewer than thirty-two questions seeking information about the applicant's family members. There were ten questions concerning the applicant's spouse, four about his or her children, seven on the applicant's parents, six on the parents-in-law, and five on the applicant's siblings.[6] Informing on one's family was required behavior in the Khmer Rouge movement.

In the section of the form devoted to parents, applicants were asked, "Do your parents have influence and power of a political, economic, material, or sentimental nature, or any kind of interaction with you? Do you have any influence or power over your parents?" In the section entitled "On Natural Children," the security forces required prospective security police and prison warders to state the sex and age of their children, how many of them were married and working, the nature of their occupations and their class membership, whether they had joined a political organization, whether they had joined the revolution, and the nature of their attitude or behavior toward the revolution.

Applicants were asked for their revolutionary views on "loving, hating, and educating children." The final question was, "Do your children have influence, power, or interaction of any kind with you?"

In this book, surviving victims hit back. They were children then. They are grown now, with memories.

Those memories include nightmares. Darkness was a constant fear, of course. But for children under the Khmer Rouge, even sleeping became one of the most terrifying aspects of life. Roeun Sam recalls, "When the night came I always worried. I stayed up even when they told us to go to sleep. Angka walked around with a flashlight at night to see who was asleep and who wasn't. I was afraid that maybe next time it will be me. I will die before I see the sun rise. I had little rest and then I heard the whistle and my head inside me sighed, 'Oh, I am alive.' I got up and got in line."

A Khmer Rouge soldier ordered children, "Go to sleep like Death." Waking up was little better. As Ouk Villa tells it, "Early in the morning all children had to get up or they were kicked and pulled by the unit leaders." The Khmer Rouge, which saw children as oppressed by their parents, expected them to behave as adults. In the words of Hong A. Chork, "My childhood was lost during those years." The Khmer Rouge allowed no time for growing up.

Another nightmare that haunted the children evacuated from the cities of Cambodia was the jungle—"the most un-safe and dangerous place in the country." The child's mind of Khuon Kiv focused on "poisonous insects, tigers, ele-phants, and dangerous snakes." The Khmer Rouge, for their part, emphasized the resources and productivity of the countryside. But the "rural areas which we never even knew existed," as Ouk Villa puts it, became a world of insecurities and fear for these youngsters. They were constantly off bal-ance. Gen L. Lee recalls, "There were times as I would smack a handful of rice plants against the side of my foot I would fall forward into the thick brown water. My body was light and I was unable to balance myself against the heavy mud. . . . When it rained, my body shivered like a tiny chick, yearning for its mother's protection and warmth. My body was reduced to bones and skin, a thin frame that could eas-ily fall when caught in the wind."

The authors of this book are mostly from Cambodia's towns. Before the revolution, urban life was more prosper-ous than in the countryside. "It was good growing up. . . . The Cambodia I knew as a child was a beautiful place," says Youkimny Chan. "My life was sheltered and well provided for," adds Gen Lee. Under the Khmer Rouge, by contrast, "it was difficult to work over ten hours a day on an empty stomach. I was not good at catching field rats and frogs. . . . Building a dam and trenches was not suited for someone under four feet."

But the stories of peasant children are often equally horrific. In March 1979, I came across two Cambodian peasant boys, aged thirteen and fourteen, who were working as unpaid servants for an official in Thailand. The boys had just escaped from the defeated Khmer Rouge army. One of them, Sat, when asked what had happened in his village in 1975 and 1976, replied, "They were killing people every day." In 1977 "all children no longer breastfeeding were taken from their parents and cared for permanently by female members of the Khmer Rouge. The reason given was to enable the mothers to work more effectively." Many of the boys Sat knew missed their parents badly. "Some of them cried with grief at times; the Khmer Rouge would beat them with sticks until they stopped crying." At the age of eleven, Sat marched off with one hundred boys to do forced labor, building a road through a jungle on the Thai border. The work was "so exhausting that some of the boys fell down unconscious at the worksite." By the time of his flight to Thailand, Sat had not seen his family for two years and did not even know whether they were alive or how to look for his home village. Sat said that when he became an adult, he wanted to "Live with other people."[8]

It is not possible to accurately assess the death toll in these children's families. Most of authors of this book lost parents, brothers, and sisters. Those whose nuclear families survived lost aunts, uncles, cousins, and grandparents. In all, about 1.7 million Cambodians died. Six million survivors saw their families decimated. And scattered. Susie Hem writes, "My mom was separated from my father. Every two months she would sneak out to meet him so they could talk about running away from this place and finding another place with more food and water."

The Khmer Rouge upended the Cambodian world in various ways. Children had to work like adults. Adults, given instructions like children, were treated like animals. Animals received better rations than workers. Adults became so alienated from the regime that young children became the only hope for the Khmer Rouge revolution to reproduce itself. Children were employed as militia, to spy on their families, and as soldiers and executioners. The Khmer Rouge hoped to use children as the basis of a new society without memory. As this books shows, that hope was fruitless. Children remained attached to their families and their memories. And in the end, the world righted itself, like the church steeple in *Great Expectations.*

Based on his readings of his parent's tombstone, Pip saw the reference to his father as "the Above" to be a sign of his lofty status. "And if any one of my deceased relations had been referred to as 'Below' I have no doubt I should have formed the worst opinions of that member of the family."[9] Death's forced separation of Cambodian children from their families had a similar impact on them. Wooden Khmer Rouge propaganda, as in the songs Angka taught them, did not diminish children's love or respect for their parents. Arn Yan, for instance, is straightforward: "I survived the Khmer Rouge largely because my mother really cared about me."

xvii

After the Vietnamese overthrow of the Pol Pot regime, a unique social revolution took place in Cambodia. Buddhism rapidly "came to itself" as the high point of village life again. And orphans all over the country immediately began putting back together their shattered families and lives. They succeeded, as this book demonstrates.

BEN KIERNAN is associate professor of history and director of the Cambodian Genocide Program at Yale University.

*Children of Cambodia's Killing Fields*

Jim Wasserman

SOPHILINE CHEAM SHAPIRO was eight when the Khmer Rouge banished her family to Kandal Province and later to Battambang Province. She returned to Phnom Penh in 1979 and enrolled at the reopened School of Fine Arts. She was a member of the first class to graduate after the Khmer Rouge regime ended, and she joined the faculty in order to help revive the Cambodian classical arts from the loss of perhaps 90 percent of their artists. With the Classical Dance Company of Cambodia she toured such countries as India, the Soviet Union, the United States, and Vietnam. In 1991, Sophiline married John Shapiro, an American, and moved to Los Angeles. Since then she has been teaching classical dance in the Los Angeles area. As the artistic director of Danse Celeste, she has performed at dance festivals, universities, and museums. Sophiline is a student in the world arts and cultures department at UCLA.

❀ ❀ ❀

# *Songs My Enemies Taught Me*

**SOPHILINE CHEAM SHAPIRO**

In April 1975 the revolutionary army of Democratic Kampuchea, commonly known as the Khmer Rouge, swept into Phnom Penh. Within weeks they had dispersed the city's population into agricultural collectives and declared history dead.

The Khmer Rouge sang about the wonderful countryside, about the value of hard labor and the worthlessness of passion. All was for Angka and the glorious revolution. They were pretty songs, with beautiful melodies and poetic lyrics. Their intention was to make us work hard and forget about the snakes that lurked in the rice paddies, the dangerous currents of river rapids, and the emptiness in our bellies. The fields were littered with bombs that exploded when struck accidentally by a hoe, and I remember watching laborers being carried off without their limbs from fields we were forced to dig.

One of the first children's songs I remember learning under the Khmer Rouge was called "Angka Dar Qotdam" (The Great Angka).

We children love Angka limitlessly.
Because of you we have better lives and live quite happily.
Before the revolution, children were poor and lived like
    animals,
We were cold and suffered,
But the enemy didn't care about us.
Only skin covered our bones, so thin we were worried.
All night we slept on the ground,
We begged and looked for food in trash cans during the
    day.
Now Angka brings us good health, strength.
And now we live in the commune.
We have clothes, we are not cold and miserable anymore.
The light of revolution, equality, and freedom shines
    gloriously.
Oh, Angka, we deeply love you.
We resolve to follow your red way.
We study hard both numbers and alphabet
To be good workers with good minds
In order to extend the revolution.

All the songs created for the new Democratic Kampuchea were filled with political references. Gone were the songs of love and heartbreak. Blood and sacrifice were the themes of the day. The Khmer Rouge's national anthem was called "Phleng Cheate":

Ruby blood that sprinkles the towns and plains
Of Kampuchea, our homeland,
Splendid blood of workers and peasants,
Splendid blood of revolutionary men and women soldiers.

The anthem ended with a glorious promise for the future:

Live, live, new Kampuchea,
Democratic and prosperous.
We resolutely lift high

The red flag of the revolution.
We build our homeland,
We cause her to progress in great leaps
In order to render her more glorious and more marvelous
    than ever.

As a nine–year–old, I believed this was the truth. There
was going to be a future, if not democratic (I don't think I
knew the meaning of that word), then one of tremendous
prosperity. Our labors continued all day, every day. We
worked from sunrise until sunset, breaking only to eat. Our
two daily meals consisted mostly of one watery cup of rice
porridge.

The lands, the forests, the villages after liberation become
    lively landscapes
With laughter everywhere.
People are enjoying their work in the villages and
    cooperatives.
They sing beautifully while they work.
Look, look at the open rice paddies,
Look further at the mature rice, like a golden carpet.
Look to the left, the young rice grows up so healthy,
Look to the right, replanted rice is growing in competition,
Look behind us, bananas compete with jackfruit, papayas
    with mangoes.
The fragrance of young and ripe fruit spreads everywhere.
In front of the houses the lemon grass, cabbage, herbs, scal-
    lions, and chilies are very green.
We are very happy living in the countryside.
We are very proud and happy.
We work hard to produce a lot more rice than before,
To improve the economy of New Kampuchea.
It is Kampuchea, independent, neutral, peaceful, advanced,
    democratic, glorious.
Men and women live in happiness.

3

We were productive, but where was the rice going? There was no democracy. There was no glory. There was no laughter. There was no happiness. By 1977 there was no more singing, and there certainly was no peace.

I sometimes wonder if images of healthy rice paddies, green chili peppers, and the wonderful new Kampuchea were whirling through the mind of my brother, Pavonn, when, dizzy from dysentery, far away from his family with a work brigade, he fainted at the top of a monastery stairwell and broke his neck. I lost my father, two brothers, my grandmother, and many cousins and uncles. I am no different from most of my generation. I know of almost no family that survived without losses. It was a time of the gravest betrayals. Lyrics that promised us the riches of heaven were written by the engineers of our own public hell.

The Vietnamese "liberated" Cambodia on January 7, 1979, sending the Khmer Rouge into hiding. The mood of the country was relatively happy. Strangers were helpful and generous with what little they had. Families wandered around the country trying to find any place that looked familiar. Some chose to cross the border into Thailand, but my family eventually returned to Phnom Penh.

I now live in the United States. One day recently I found myself on a bus contemplating the way that each of the political factions under which I have lived has taught me one thing, only to have the next regime tell me something completely different. This constant change in ideology has left me, and I think my whole generation, confused. We are left to search through the rubble and find some truth for ourselves.

I rarely hear the songs of the Khmer Rouge. I wonder why that is. I know all too well the horror their melodies recall, but I also know that these songs played as important a part in my life as any. They reflect an experience unique to my generation of Cambodians, no matter to what corner of the world fate has brought them. The Khmer Rouge hoped to obliterate our history, and in doing so, their songs have forged a significant place in it. It is for this reason that I will never forget the songs my enemies taught me.

CHATH PIERSATH in 1979 crossed the Thai-Cambodian border with his second oldest sister and second oldest brother on foot to Aranyaprathet Refugee Camp. His brother was able to go to America with his aunt, who later sponsored Chath and his sister with the help of the Presbyterian Church. They arrived in Boulder, Colorado, in 1981. After moving to California he graduated from the World College West in Petaluma with a bachelor's degree in international service and development. Chath went back to Cambodia to work for the Cambodian American National Development Organization (CANDO) as a volunteer. He was a consultant to local nongovernmental organizations working with human rights, HIV/AIDS education, street children, and rural development. He plans to return to his home province to help people there.

❀ ❀ ❀

# *A Letter to My Mother*

**CHATH PIERSATH**

Waiting is all I can do to lay flowers down on your grave,
to say good–bye, to embrace you one last time, and to
present myself to you and show you how I am, your son.

My eyes, Mother, are much like yours, full of tears.
My hands are fencing and fighting away those dark
    dreams.
My complexion is collecting dust, aiming for the sky with
the hope that one day I will come to understand the ways
of the world, how it works.

I see you in the distance, limping home, half–crippled,
on an empty dirt road looking for your children.
The Khmer Rouge had taken them away.
Your boys were taken to Angka to do slave labor.
For five years there was no news of them.
You didn't know where your eldest son and his family were.
I was the only son left to watch you soliciting answers to
questions about a war you could not win.
Like other mothers, you tried to wage a battle against it
with the intention of saving what was left of your children.

I remember you calling my name while I sat on a tree
    eating leaves.

I tried begging for rice, but the men who were eating did
    not care.
They turned their backs and laughed while I stood
    watching them eat.
I wanted to stay on that tree and fall down among the
    foliage of tears, rotten and free of suffering.

But your assurance stretching out your fine, stick–like
    hands peeled me down from my hungry embrace.
Like the tree receiving the sun and rain as its sustenance,
I took your delicate tears and words as my food.

Oh, Mother, I am grateful to you, for your sorrowful
    strength and your woman's instinct to preserve life and
    the dignity of your womb.

In spite of the hunger, you kept on living, chanting prayers,
    calling upon the spirit of your dead husband, invoking
    your ancestors and your deity to pour rain on earth, to
    stop the war and stop others from rearranging your fate,
    deranging your children, and disarranging your home.

I had feared, Mother, when you became gaunt and frail,
    that you would leave me orphaned in that mad country
    with a two–year–old sister dying of starvation.

There was no rice on our plates, and you had become ill.
I went around begging and gathering whatever I could
to keep you breathing, praying, and calling the spirits.
You did not give up.
You lived to see the return of your missing children.
The Vietnamese came dropping bombs, rolling in their tanks
and ammunitions in 1979. You were on the Khmer Rouge's
torture list, but the Vietnamese saved you as the sound
of their bombardment chased Pol Pot's bloodthirsty army
away.

But again, your children left you. Three went to the United States. One was killed by the Khmer Rouge. One is living in a refugee camp in that selfish Thailand. The grand-children you knew starved to death, and the ones you never met are wishing your presence. One son is missing. Two daughters stayed by your side when you left them. You left us who have never said good-bye or laid a single flower on your grave.

It has been seventeen years. Forgive me, Mother, for my long absence.

TEEDA BUTT MAM *is the mother of two and now a U.S. citizen. She works in the computer software industry and lives in California's Silicon Valley. She keeps abreast of developments in her former homeland and is actively involved in the Cambodian American community. Two books have been published about her experiences:* To Destroy You Is No Loss *and* Bamboo & Butterflies: From Refugee to Citizen, *both published by East/West Bridge Publishing House, Dixon, California, and written by JoAn D. Criddle.*

❀ ❀ ❀

# Worms from Our Skin

## TEEDA BUTT MAM

I was fifteen years old when the Khmer Rouge came to power in April 1975. I can still remember how overwhelmed with joy I was that the war had finally ended.

It did not matter who won. I and many Cambodians wanted peace at any price. The civil war had tired us out, and we could not make much sense out of killing our own brothers and sisters for a cause that was not ours. We were ready to support our new government to rebuild our country. We wanted to bring back that slow-paced, simple life we grew up with and loved dearly. At the time we didn't realize how high the price was that we had to pay for the Khmer Rouge's peace.

The Khmer Rouge were very clever and brutal. Their tactics were effective because most of us refused to believe their malicious intentions. Their goal was to liberate us. They risked their own lives and gave up their families for "justice" and "equality." How could these worms have come out of our own skin?

Even after our warmest welcome, the first word from the Khmer Rouge was a lie wrapped around a deep anger and hatred of the kind of society they felt Cambodia was becoming. They told us that Americans were going to bomb the cities. They forced millions of residents of Phnom Penh and other cities out of their homes. They separated us from our friends and neighbors to keep us off balance, to prevent us from forming any alliance to stand up and win back our rights. They ripped off our homes and our possessions. They did this intentionally, without mercy.

They were willing to pay any cost, any lost lives for their mission. Innocent children, old women, and sick patients from hospital beds were included. Along the way, many innocent Cambodians were dying of starvation, disease, loss of loved ones, confusion, and execution.

We were seduced into returning to our hometowns in the villages so they could reveal our true identities. Then the genocide began. First, it was the men.

They took my father. They told my family that my father needed to be reeducated. Brainwashed. But my father's fate is unknown to this day. We can only imagine what happened to him. This is true for almost all Cambodian widows and orphans. We live in fear of finding out what atrocities were committed against our fathers, husbands, brothers. What could they have done that deserved a tortured death?

Later the Khmer Rouge killed the wives and children of the executed men in order to avoid revenge. They encouraged children to find fault with their own parents and spy on them. They openly showed their intention to destroy the family structure that once held love, faith, comfort, happiness, and companionship. They took young children from their homes to live in a commune so that they could indoctrinate them.

Parents lost their children. Families were separated. We were not allowed to cry or show any grief when they took away our loved ones. A man would be killed if he lost an ox he was assigned to tend. A woman would be killed if she was too tired to work. Human life wasn't even worth a bullet. They clubbed the back of our necks and pushed us down to smother us and let us die in a deep hole with hundreds of other bodies.

They told us we were VOID. We were less than a grain of rice in a large pile. The Khmer Rouge said that the Communist revolution could be successful with only two people. Our lives had no significance to their great Communist nation, and they told us, "To keep you is no benefit, to destroy you is no loss."

They accomplished all of this by promoting and encouraging the "old" people, who were the villagers, the farmers, and the uneducated. They were the most violent and ignorant people, and the Khmer Rouge taught them to lead, manage, control, and destroy. These people took orders without question. The Khmer Rouge built animosity and jealousy into them so the killings could be justified. They ordered us to attend meetings every night where we took turns finding fault with each other, intimidating those around us. We survived by becoming like them. We stole, we cheated, we lied, we hated ourselves and each other, and we trusted no one.

The people on the Khmer Rouge death list were the group called the city people. They were the "new" people. These were any Cambodian men, women, girls, boys, and babies who did not live in their "liberated zones" before they won the war in 1975. Their crime was that they lived in the enemy's zone, helping and supporting the enemy.

The city people were the enemy, and the list was long. Former soldiers, the police, the CIA, and the KGB. Their crime was fighting in the civil war. The merchants, the capitalists, and the businessmen. Their crime was exploiting the poor. The rich farmers and the landlords. Their crime was exploiting the peasants. The intellectuals, the doctors, the lawyers, the monks, the teachers, and the civil servants. These people thought, and their memories were tainted by the evil Westerners. Students were getting education to exploit the poor. Former celebrities, the poets. These people carried bad memories of the old, corrupted Cambodia.

The list goes on and on. The rebellious, the kind–hearted, the brave, the clever, the individualists, the people who wore glasses, the literate, the popular, the complainers, the lazy, those with talent, those with trouble getting along with others, and those with soft hands. These people were corrupted and lived off the blood and sweat of the farmers and the poor.

Very few of us escaped these categories. My family were not villagers. We were from Phnom Penh. I was afraid of who I was. I was an educated girl from a middle–class family. I could read, write, and think. I was proud of my family and my roots. I was scared that they would hear my thoughts and prayers, that they could see my dreams and feel my anger and disapproval of their regime.

I was always hungry. I woke up hungry before sunrise and walked many kilometers to the worksite with no breakfast. I worked until noon. My lunch was either rice porridge with a few grains or boiled young bananas or boiled corn. I continued working till sunset. My dinner was the same as lunch. I couldn't protest to Angka, but my stomach protested to me that it needed more food. Every night I went to sleep dirty and hungry. I was sad because I missed my mom. I was fearful that this might be the night I'd be taken away, tortured, raped, and killed.

I wanted to commit suicide but I couldn't. If I did, I would be labeled "the enemy" because I dared to show my unhappiness with their regime. My death would be followed by my family's death because they were the family of the enemy. My greatest fear was not my death, but how much suffering I had to go through before they killed me.

They kept moving us around, from the fields into the woods. They purposely did this to disorient us so they could have complete control. They did it to get rid of the "useless people." Those who were too old or too weak to work. Those who did not produce their quota. We were cold because we had so few clothes and blankets. We had no shoes. We were sick and had little or no medical care. They told us that we "volunteered" to work fifteen hours or more a day in the rain or in the moonlight with no holidays. We were timid and lost. We had to be silent. We not only lost our identities, but we lost our pride, our senses, our religion, our loved ones, our souls, ourselves.

The Khmer Rouge said they were creating a utopian nation where everyone would be equal. They restarted our nation by resettling everyone and changing everything back to zero. The whole nation was equally poor. But while the entire population was dying of starvation, disease, and hopelessness, the Khmer Rouge was creating a new upper class. Their soldiers and the Communist party members were able to choose any woman or man they wanted to marry. In addition to boundless food, they were crazed with gold, jewelry, perfume, imported watches, Western medicine, cars, motorcycles, bicycles, silk, and other imported goods.

My dear friend Sakon was married to a handicapped Khmer Rouge veteran against her will. He was mentally disturbed and also suffered from tetanus. At night he woke up from his sleep with nightmares of his crimes and his killings. After that, he beat her. One night, he stabbed my friend to death and injured her mother.

Near my hut there was a woman named Chamroeun. She watched her three children die of starvation, one at a time. She would have been able to save their lives had she had gold or silk or perfume to trade for food and medicine on the black market. The Khmer Rouge veterans and village leaders had control of the black market. They traded rice that Chamroeun toiled over for fancy possessions. The Khmer Rouge gave a new meaning to corruption.

The female soldiers were jealous of my lighter skin and feminine figure. While they were enjoying their nice black pajamas, silk scarves, jewelry, new shoes, and perfume, they stared at me, seeing if I had anything better than they did. I tried to appear timid with my ragged clothes, but it was hard to hide the pride in my eyes.

In January 1979 I was called to join a district meeting. The district leader told us that it was time to get rid of "all the wheat that grows among the rice plants." The city people were the wheat. The city people were to be eliminated. My life was saved because the Vietnamese invasion came just two weeks later.

When the Vietnamese invasion happened, I cried. I was crying with joy that my life was saved. I was crying with sorrow that my country was once again invaded by our century-old enemy. I stood on Cambodian soil feeling that I no longer belonged to it. I wanted freedom. I decided to escape to the free world.

I traveled with my family from the heart of the country to the border of Thailand. It was devastating to witness the destruction of my homeland that had occurred in only four years. Buddhist temples were turned into prisons. Statues of Buddha and artwork were vandalized. Schools were turned into Khmer Rouge headquarters where people were inter-rogated, tortured, killed, and buried. School yards were turned into killing fields. Old marketplaces were empty. Books were burned. Factories were left to rust. Plantations were without tending and bore no fruit.

This destruction was tolerable compared to the human conditions. Each highway was filled with refugees. We were refugees of our own country. With our skinny bodies, bloated stomachs, and hollow eyes, we carried our few possessions and looked for our separated family members. We asked who lived and didn't want to mention who died. We gath-ered to share our horrifying stories. Stories about people being pushed into deep wells and ponds and suffocating to death. People were baked alive in a local tile oven. One woman was forced to cook her husband's liver, which was cut out while he was still alive. Women were raped before execution. One old man said, "It takes a river of ink to write our stories."

In April 1979, the Buddhist New Year, exactly four years after the Khmer Rouge came to power, I joined a group of corpselike bodies dancing freely to the sound of clapping and songs of folk music that defined who we were. We danced under the moonlight around the bonfire. We were celebrating the miracles that saved our lives. At that moment, I felt that my spirit and my soul had returned to my weak body. Once again, I was human.

*YOUKIMNY CHAN was sponsored in 1980 by Catholic Social Services in Rochester, Minnesota, where he lived until he completed his education. He received a bachelor of science degree in social work from Winona State University, Winona, Minnesota. He lives in Long Beach, California, where he is a children's social worker with the Los Angeles Department of Children and Family Services. Youkimny's story was written with the generous help of Jean Carroll, an English teacher in Rochester, Minnesota.*

✿  ✿  ✿

# One Spoon of Rice

### YOUKIMNY CHAN

**W**hen I was just a little boy I would sit with my sister Sin-
uoen in our swing under a coconut tree. She would read stories to me about amazing places. We would talk and sing songs
together and sometimes listen to soap operas on the radio. I
loved my sister and I loved those happy times we spent together. In the evenings we would sit under the full moon and
listen to the crickets and the coconut tree leaves rustling in the
breeze. We would talk about what we wanted to do when we
grew up. It was good growing up in Cambodia.

In the afternoon, while the adults napped, the children
would go down to the river to swim. The beaches of the Mekong River were wide and sandy, and the river was blue and
sparkling. My friends and I would splash and yell and then
run onto the beach and start a game of soccer or hopscotch or
volleyball. If we got hungry, there were always fruit trees
nearby, heavy with mangos, coconuts, and bananas. The Cambodia I knew as a child was a beautiful place. Things grew
quickly there. Hibiscus and roses of all colors filled the air with
fragrance. My grandmother would bring armfuls of flowers
into our house every day. We lived in a garden. When I close
my eyes I can still see the blue skies and the tropical flowers.
I can still see the laughing faces of my friends and family.

My family was very close. My father, who was a captain
in the Cambodian army, had died of malaria when I was
three years old, but my grandparents took me, my mother,
and my brothers and sisters to live with them. They became
my second parents. I always thought of my grandfather as
my real father. Although he was gone often, when he was at
home he made time for his grandchildren. I respected him

and loved him deeply. My mother was a professional nurse and was very respected by people who knew her.

My oldest sister, Sinoy, was already married and had three children. My brother Kimhour, who was seven years older than I, was a student at the University of Cambodia and a well-known soccer player. My favorite sibling was Sin-uoen, who was five years older than I. She was always patient with me. The youngest in my family was my little brother, Sombo. With my grandparents, we lived in a very large house that had been in the family for generations. It was a beautiful house and it had wonderful black hardwood floors. My grandmother was so proud of those shiny floors. She waxed them every day with coconut skins, kerosene, and candle wax to make them glow.

In 1974 the Khmer Rouge took over all the small villages surrounding Phnom Penh, as my grandfather predicted. Soon after that, the bombing of our city began. When the shelling of Phnom Penh started, we were frightened, but we were also a little relieved. We knew that the war would soon be over. Many people from the small towns around us had fled to Phnom Penh as their villages were attacked and destroyed. Many of them had nowhere to live, and so they slept in the streets.

On April 17, 1975, when I was fourteen years old, the Khmer Rouge army came into Phnom Penh with tanks. A man in a slow-moving car shouting into a loudspeaker ordered all the police and military leaders to put down their guns and surrender. He told all the people to leave their houses. My grandfather didn't want the Khmer Rouge to know he was a military officer for their enemy, so he hid his uniform and weapons. We wouldn't leave the house. It was our home, and we were free people. We were not about to let anyone tell us to leave.

Then soldiers came to our house with their guns and ordered us to leave. They said we would be gone for only three days, and during that time the Khmer Rouge would clean up the city so that it would be safe for us to return. But the soldiers came again and said that the American B-52 bombers were going to attack the city and that we would have to leave in a hurry or be killed by their bombs. The soldiers assured us that they would defeat the Americans and that then we could return to our homes.

These soldiers were our countrymen. We had no reason not to believe them. They weren't going to let us get hurt. So we packed our car with clothes, some gold and jewelry, and some food. Everyone in my family left together. Some crowded into the car and the rest of us walked. Leaving Phnom Penh was an adventure. Thousands of people were leaving at the same time. The streets and sidewalks were covered with people carrying bags, and cars crept along slowly in the congestion. There was so much noise.

The next day, soldiers came and searched us. They took our jewelry, our car, and most of our clothes. Now everyone in our family had to walk, and we had to divide the remaining food among us to carry it on our backs. It was the dry season and it was very hot. There was no water. People began to get heatstroke and fall down on the road. The soldiers wouldn't let us stop to help those who were sick. I couldn't believe what was happening. We walked for days, then weeks. Pregnant women gave birth under trees by the road. Old people died from exhaustion and lack of water. Everywhere was the sound of babies screaming and people crying for loved ones who had died and had to be left on the road.

There was no time for funerals. Soldiers threw the bodies into empty ponds and kept everyone moving. Guns were pointed at us, and tanks forced us to keep moving. I saw two men with their hands tied behind their backs. Soldiers were questioning them on the side of the road. The soldiers cut off the men's heads, which fell to the ground as their bodies slumped. There was nothing I could do. People were being murdered before my eyes. These were my friends, my neighbors. The rest of us kept walking.

Finally, after almost two and a half months of walking and stopping, walking and stopping, we arrived outside the province of Battambang, where most of the small villages in the jungle had been burned to ashes during the fighting. We

❀
21

were told that we must live in those burned-out villages. We were civilized people. We had never lived in the jungle without houses and electricity and running water. We still believed that we would be allowed to return home. My grandfather asked the soldiers when we would leave and was told, "In a few days." After many days, I saw him beginning to lose faith.

Our family had to survive even though we had almost nothing. My grandfather, older brother, and brother-in-law built a small hut out of bamboo they cut down. It had a bamboo floor to protect us from snakes and palm leaves for the roof. Thirteen of us lived together in the hut.

All of us started to get sick from malnutrition. Many were getting malaria. There was no medicine and no doctors. Finally we began to eat banana and papaya trees—not the fruit of the trees. We would peel off some layers of the bark, then cut off pieces of the tree and boil them with salt. It gave us something to eat, but it also made some of my family very sick. My sister's ten-year-old son got diarrhea and died after three days of suffering. Then her seven-year-old daughter died. My sister went crazy with grief. She would not move from the spot where we buried them. She never recovered.

After we had been in our hut for about a year, the soldiers came to take my grandfather. They grabbed him and tied his hands behind his back. "We know you were in the military," they said to him. Grandfather did not struggle. But as he left, he turned to my grandmother and said, "Would you take care of my family?" The soldiers slapped him in the face and marched him out. Many minutes went by. We heard a shot deep in the jungle. We knew Grandfather was dead.

The Khmer Rouge continued their killing. If someone was suspected of having an education or of being an intellectual, the soldiers would pull him out of his hut at night and shoot him or cut his throat. None of us could ask questions or cry out. We were weak and sick. We had no weapons. And if we made the soldiers angry, they would kill us.

Three months after my grandfather was murdered, the soldiers took my brother and brother-in-law. They were tied up and taken two or three miles into the jungle. This time I followed, sneaking through the undergrowth so that no one would see me. I watched as my brothers were forced to dig a large hole while the soldiers held guns to their heads. I remember one soldier saying to the other, "We will save our bullets." Then they took big bamboo shoots and beat my brothers again and again until they were dead. Their bodies were kicked into the hole. Their grave was not far from where my grandfather was killed.

Those who were not murdered by the soldiers were dying a slow death. We traded what little we had been able to hide for food from a government family. An ounce of gold would get us a cup of rice. Soon we had nothing left to trade. We were always hungry. We were always sick. My oldest sister, Sinoy, could no longer talk or move. After about a year of living in the jungle, one of my mother's sisters, who had been living with us, died early in the morning. Soon after, my other aunt died. We found her body already stiff when we woke one morning. The neighbors helped us bury them but we had no grave markers. So many had been buried around the village that it was impossible to keep track of the burial places. By the next day, we couldn't tell where their graves were.

Within about three months after the deaths of my aunts, my grandmother died, and then my older sister. She had already buried her husband and children, and she had nothing to live for. The rest of us continued to struggle to survive. Whenever we got some food, we would divide it. My mother would always give me part of hers. I was her favorite child, and she wanted me to live. But now my mother was very sick. I was afraid she was dying.

She spoke to me quietly. "Son, if you ever get away from the Communists, go to school. They can take away your possessions, but they can't take your education. They can't take what you know." Soon after that, my mother died. I wanted to die, too. She had always taken care of me and I had depended on her. Now there was no one to take care of me. Soon my little brother died. The neighbors helped me bury him. Now only my sister and I remained.

My favorite sister, Sinuoen, continued to get weaker and

weaker. Her skin was sticking to her bones, and she had lost her long black hair. I think this was the hardest time of all for me. It was my responsibility as the oldest male to protect my sister. My mother would be counting on me. But there was nothing I could do. And one day, as we sat together in the hut, Sinuoen put her head on my lap and said, "Kimny, I don't know if I can live any longer. Can I have a spoon of rice?"

My heart was breaking. It was such a little thing she asked. But we had no rice. I got up and brought her our last cup of water. "Sister," I said, "I have no rice to give you. Drink this water." She looked into my face for a moment, and then she sipped the water. She put her head down on my lap. And then she died.

I don't know why I didn't die, too. I didn't want to live any more. I was so tired and so hungry. I wandered around for months after that begging for a bit of rice from anyone who had some. I never went back to our hut. Sometimes I slept outside. Sometimes I crawled into the hut of another family. But most families had suffered like mine. No one had enough food. No one had hope.

Then the Khmer Rouge decided they needed more young people from the villages to work for them. They took all the teenagers from our jungle village to a concentration camp in the jungle about thirty miles from where my new hut was. I wasn't afraid to go. My family was all gone. I thought, "If I walk and drop dead, I'll drop dead. It's not so bad."

The concentration camp was just a clearing in the jungle. The other young prisoners and I built a makeshift hut with the bamboo we found. We worked from sunrise to sunset, fourteen or fifteen hours a day, in the rice paddies. It was the rainy season, and the work was hard. After a whole day's work we would be fed a few bites of dry fish and a little rice. Then, before we could sleep, the Khmer Rouge would lecture us about how to be good Communists. They said that Pol Pot was our Angka. Pol Pot was our new family. If any of us found that our parents were not obeying the Communists, we should turn them in.

We could not escape. The camp was encircled by barbed wire, and the thousand or so of us were all afraid for our lives. Sometimes they would pull a boy out of his hut at night and we wouldn't see him again. Sometimes they would take a boy into the jungle and we would hear him scream. Sometimes they would throw the body parts of a boy they had cut apart into the rice paddies as we worked. "Fertilizer," they would say.

When I was about seventeen years old, I remember trying to sleep at night but the sound of bombing in the distance kept me awake. Each night the bombing got closer and closer. We found out later that the Vietnamese were pushing the Khmer Rouge out of our area and up against the Thai border. The Khmer Rouge guards never said anything about the fighting.

Then one day the Vietnamese soldiers entered our camp. At first, we didn't know who they were. But when they began speaking to us, some of the boys recognized their language. We discovered that the Cambodian soldiers had all deserted the camp. The Vietnamese were kind to us but they told us to leave. We had hoped and prayed to leave for years, and now that we had the chance, we realized that we had nowhere to go. I left the camp with Savath, my new friend. We headed toward Battambang and luckily my friend met up with his family. Houses did not have electricity or running water. The hospitals, schools, and markets were closed. Food was still scarce.

When I was eighteen I felt I had to return to Phnom Penh to see if any of my cousins or friends had survived Pol Pot. My house was more than one hundred twenty kilometers from Battambang, and I didn't know the way. I started walking in that general direction. I got on an old train, got rides on wagons, and walked some more. Eventually I arrived in Phnom Penh. As I entered my old neighborhood, my spirit crumbled. My house was burned and my friends' houses were burned. Everything that had once been so familiar was gone. I knew that my life was changed forever.

*SOPHEAP K. HANG was six when the Khmer Rouge took power. In 1981 she was sponsored by her mother's relatives. She came to the United States from a Red Cross refugee camp in Thailand and now lives in Santa Rosa, California. She recently graduated with a bachelor of arts degree in Mexican American multicultural studies from Sonoma State University. She teaches middle school in San Francisco.*

❀ ❀ ❀

# Memoir of a Child's Nightmare

## SOPHEAP K. HANG

$B$eing a young child, I asked my mother why we couldn't play on the front porch. She looked at me not in an angry way, but in a frightened and fearful way. I didn't know why my mother acted the way she did. Afterward, she went to the kitchen to look for boxes, and she found a few near the cabinet. She then took out bags of rice, salt, sugar, pans, pots, plates, and utensils and put them in a box. She went to Sophear and Makara's bedroom. She took their clothes and put them in a box. Then my mother approached my bedroom, which was located on the left side of the kitchen, and she took my clothes. She put them in a box.

My mother turned toward us children and said, "Don't go out to play this week. Just stay inside the house so I can keep an eye on all of you, okay?" We all nodded our heads. I looked at my mother with a questioning look. I didn't dare ask her why because it's very impolite to question elders. Sophear and I looked at each other with questioning eyes.

The next morning I heard loud noises coming from the street. I looked out my window. I saw a jeep with three soldiers in it. Then came four or five other trucks, full of young soldiers carrying guns and waving white flags, shouting "Victory! Victory! Victory!" The people were jumping, laughing, hopping, waving white flags, and singing and dancing around the army trucks.

Within an instant I heard gunshots—BANG! BANG! BANG!—
from the front jeep. One soldier stood up with his gun
pointed to the sky. He fired a shot because he wanted to get
people's attention. The announcement was made over the
megaphone, "Cambodia needs to be reconstructed. We need
the citizens of Cambodia to leave their homes for a couple of
days. We need the time to reestablish the new government
for better prosperity. You have to move out NOW." BANG! BANG!
A man was shot.

My mother grabbed me from the window. I was numb
from my head to my toes by the horrifying action of the soldier. The man was face down. Both of his hands were twisted
on top of his back. His face was smashed against the cement.
Blood was everywhere. My mother shook me very hard until I came out of my bewilderment.

My father took the supplies my mother packed and put
them in a wagon he had built. I looked out the window again.
I saw a very young soldier, around fifteen or sixteen years
old, accost my father. After the conversation my father rushed
inside to hurry his parents, my mother, and the children out
of the house.

We were evacuated from our home on April 17, a very
dusty, hot, and humid day. Thousands and thousands of Cambodian people were forced out of their homes. During the
evacuation the city of Cambodia was crowded with people,
automobiles, animals, and abandoned children. Sip, sip,
plop, plop . . . beep, beep . . . waaa, waaa . . . The sounds of
feet, babies crying, and car engines surrounded us as we
were forced out of the city. Children were crying because
they were being separated from their parents. Some were
crying because their parents had abandoned them. The streets
were full of thousands and thousands of frightened people
running and shouting for lost ones. Many of their belongings were left behind. Elderly people were forced out of their
homes with only the clothes on their bodies.

I remember my mother holding Makara on her hip and

holding Sophear with her other hand. I was holding onto my mother's leg. I had never walked such a long distance before. Tears burst out of my eyes, but not a single sound came out of my mouth. I forced myself to walk miles and miles away from the city. I knew that Sophear was in the same painful position as I was. My mother kept looking back to see if I was okay. She didn't worry much about herself, even though she carried Makara and held Sophear's hand, along with a few packs on her back.

Several days passed. The city was annihilated by the new government and was emptied. Its soul was destroyed. Houses and tall buildings stood there with no spirit. It became a ghost town in the flash of a few seconds.

After a long walk the soldiers told the people to find a place to rest. My father found a spot under a coconut tree. My mother helped my father lay out a bamboo mat. I was tired from walking. I found myself a flat spot on the mat and plopped on it. I looked down at my feet. I had blisters everywhere. My mother asked me if I was hurt. I told her I was okay, but she looked at my feet and knew that I wasn't telling the truth. She told me it was going to be all right. She brought me to a nearby stream so I could relax my feet in the cold water.

Many more days passed. The soldiers started to call families in for new registration cards. One man who was in line told the soldiers that he was a professor at the Cambodian University. His family was taken to the reeducation institution. My father somehow knew this government wasn't going to be safe and trustworthy anymore. My father told us not to call him "Pa" and my mother "Mak" anymore. He took my French books and some of the photos we had taken on special occasions and burned them. I didn't know why he did it, but if the soldiers knew, he would have been scolded.

My family was called to give our true identifications. My father told the soldier his name and his occupation. "I'm a farmer. I am an agricultural man, nothing special. I lived in

❀

29

the city because I wanted to make an easy living by selling vegetables." My father had to pretend that he was an ignorant man. The soldier didn't believe my father at first, but then my mother took out a photo from her documentary film on Cambodian agricultural women (a film my parents produced for the French people). My mother was dressed in farmer's clothing and planting rice in one of the pictures. She showed it to the soldier. He accepted the photo as evidence that my parents were farmers.

My family survived this first round of questioning. We were put with the farm people. My parents told Sophear, Makara, and me not to say anything about our true identities. My mother wanted her children to conform to our new identities. I shook my head back and forth because I didn't know what "identities" meant. Then someone said, "Plant a deaf tree in front of oneself, if one wants to survive," meaning that if I wanted to stay alive, I had to act deaf and say nothing.

When the registration of the remaining people was over, a leader of Angka showed up. He stood before the people holding a microphone in one hand. He gathered the new people to listen to his speech. "I am the new leader of Cambodia. From now on you have to address the new government as Angka. There are no homes for you to return to. You have to work as a group from now on. No one can own property. Everything you own belongs to Angka. No more city lifestyle. Everyone has to dress in black uniforms." My mother looked at my father with concern. "No one can question Angka," he said. "If you have courage to question Angka, you will be taken to the reeducation learning institution." That meant we would be executed. Everyone, including my parents, was numb. We could not think. Our bodies were shaking and our minds were paralyzed by the imposing speech of Angka.

Things didn't get any better. Angka told my parents and the people of Cambodia to work in the fields, plant rice crops, dig ditches, build riverbanks, and plow the fields. My parents worked from sunrise to sunset for a spoonful of rice to fill their stomachs. Angka treated people worse than animals. Every morning the fields were covered by black ants, working their way around for food. Some of us were digging ditches and some were plowing, planting rice seed, and building riverbanks. When it was time for lunch, the bell rang and everyone disappeared from the field into the meal lines, waiting for their portion.

Many months passed by. Things got harder and harder. Angka made the city people work from early dawn to midnight. The food portion was cut to half a spoon of rice and half a spoon of green beans. The city people couldn't stand the suffering and the torture that Angka forced on them. Some of them committed suicide by hanging from trees, strangling themselves with ropes around their necks, or by suffocation.

During this time I saw the most horrible incident in my entire life. It happened around midafternoon. My mother and father were away at work. Sophear and Makara were asleep. I heard voices coming from my neighbor's house. I heard a crying voice, begging and pleading for forgiveness. A man shouted, "No! No! I must set a good example for the city people." Smack! Slam! The man was on the ground and a woman was kneeling beside the Khmer Rouge soldier, asking for forgiveness. The soldier made the man grovel around him. Then he asked the man's wife to stand him up. The soldier took the man's hands and twisted them behind his back, tying them with a rope.

The soldier shoved the man out of the house and took him to the riverbank. He tied him up against a tree. The man was exhausted from the beating and he collapsed against the tree, unconscious. I was scared from the incident. I was so worried that the soldier might see me watching him torture this innocent man. I squatted in the corner of my bamboo house, shaking. My mouth shivered and I couldn't stop myself from trembling, so I hugged my knees against my chest for comfort. There I waited for my parents to return from work.

When my mother arrived, she was tired and looked fearful. She sat on the bamboo bed and looked at me. "Did you take good care of your brother and sister and the village children?" I told her yes. My job was to take care of the village children while their parents were away working. I had to feed them, change their ragged cloth diapers, give them baths, and sing to them. I also had to water the vegetable garden, going down to the river and back, carrying the heavy water.

I looked into my mother's eyes and I told her what I saw that afternoon. My mother became stiff. She couldn't move her jaw muscles. She kept looking at me for a few minutes. Then she told me not to mention the incident to anyone. That night the man was killed by two gunshots. Angka killed him because he was an educated man. He was caught reading a letter from his poor mother. The sound of bullets made me squirm. My mother held me close when the second shot went off. I tried to close my eyes and my ears at the same time to protect myself from hearing the shots.

The next morning, Mother told me not to go by the tree. I was a stubborn child so I went to the tree by the riverbank to see the man's body. The body wasn't there, but there were pieces of his skin, hair, and blood attached to the tree. Blood was spread everywhere under the tree. Suddenly my body began to shake, and the blood made me sick to my stomach. I threw up on the tree. Then I ran home as fast as I could without looking back. I was sick for at least a month over it. This incident happened when I was around eight years old. This was just one of the many terrible things that I saw. It's too painful to reveal any others.

I will never forget what happened to that innocent man. Recently I told my mother that I went to the tree by the riverbank where the man was killed. I told her what I saw. She looked at me and told me, "That's why. I couldn't figure out why you were sick for the whole month." Mother and I began laughing, but then the memory hit our hearts. We burst into tears.

Sometimes it's frightening for me to look back at my past experiences. Once in a while I wonder about my uncles and how they were killed. It is very hard for Cambodians to let their memories go.

SREYTOUCH SVAY-RYSER *and her family lived in Cambodia until 1980. Her mother was able to gather the surviving members of her family and leave for Khao-I-Dang refugee camp in Thailand. They were sponsored to the United States in 1981 by one of Sreytouch's older sisters and a local church organization. Her family settled in Olympia, Washington, where she started attending school at the age of thirteen. Since graduating from high school Sreytouch has worked for an insurance company and the state of Washington while attending a local community college. She works for the Washington State Parks and Recreation Commission as the secretary for a regional engineering office. Since arriving in the United States her family members have found stable jobs and had wonderful families of their own.*

❀ ❀ ❀

# New Year's Surprise

### SREYTOUCH SVAY-RYSER

On April 16, 1975, I was only seven and was living with my older sister Sandy and her husband, Kunth, in Phnom Penh. Something happened. I heard an explosion and gun- fire. Someone got shot, and it was our neighbor, who was always too outspoken. I was told to stay in the house. We didn't have any television, so we couldn't hear any broad- casts. The gunfire stopped a while later.

The next morning we packed our new clothes and got ready to go to my oldest sister's house, where my family was meeting for the New Year's celebration. We left pretty early on my brother-in-law's Vespa. It carried five people: my older brother, Sandy, the baby, Kunth, and me. It would be a fun day and I was looking forward to the New Year.

At my sister's house everyone was busy preparing food and trying to get the last-minute items done. My sisters Boran and Chharvy were sent back to my house because we had forgotten some gifts. It wasn't too far away, so they hopped up on the scooter. Somewhere during that time a broadcast came on the radio saying that we should come out and help celebrate Independence Day. Soon after the broad- cast a tank roared past our front door. Another radio broad- cast said that the country had fallen to the Pol Pot regime, and they announced that certain roads would be closed at noon. It was almost noon already, and my family began to panic because Boran and Chharvy had not made it back yet.

My family didn't know what else to do, so the children were told to get ready for the celebration and to take their showers. My niece, Lynn, and I were the last to take our showers. Before we could finish, a disturbance was heard in the street. My brother–in–law Toun went to lock the front gate. It wasn't long after that when eight to twelve young men in black uniforms formed two rows outside our front gate. With their guns pointing at us, they told us to open the gate because they wanted to check for missing weapons. We didn't open the gate. They yelled again for us to open the gate or they'd shoot us. My brother–in–law used one of my mother's white blouses, which was hanging outside to dry, and raised it like a flag. Then we watched my brother–in–law open the gate.

My dad went to grab both Lynn and me out of the shower. We had only shorts on. Lynn was only six years old at the time. We both were scared to death, but so was everyone else.

My two sisters still hadn't come back. We were told to get out of the house for a few hours so they could check it. We asked if we could go upstairs and pack a few things, but the answer was NO! We left the house with just what we had on. Both my niece and I had no shirts or shoes. We were told to follow the crowds and to go in only one direction. We walked and walked in the blistering hot sunny day. My feet were killing me. The melting tar was too hot for my little feet. My dad found brown paper bags and, with rubber bands from our hair, he tied the bags around our feet to protect them. It was a very long walk.

We finally reached the village we were assigned to. Life was rough there. Three of my unmarried sisters (thirteen to sixteen years of age) were taken away to a labor camp. We hardly ever saw them after that. They worked from sunrise to sunset with a minimum amount of food in their stomachs. Everyone else worked about the same schedule. We were supposed to clear the land of mines so we could farm. Every day someone was getting killed by the mines. Coming from city life, people weren't expected to do farming. My parents told us that we can't tell anyone that our father and brother-in-law were in the military or that my other brother-in-law was a doctor. We were told to say that our whole family came from a village and that all we ever had done was farming.

Before my oldest sister, Tavy, passed away, she went into a coma during the night. My family gathered together. In the morning, Angka came to our house and told us to bury my sister and get to work. We begged them to let us be with her and told them that she wasn't dead yet. She died later that morning, leaving behind her husband and three small children.

It wasn't too long after my sister's death that Tavy's husband got sick and became delirious. He went around the neighborhood asking if anyone had seen his wife. He died later that year. Tavy and Toun's older son died before Toun did. Their youngest son, Pharack, also became sick. While we were all at work, Pharack was supposed to be at home. We came home and couldn't find him anywhere. A lady found him late at night wandering around, crying and eating garbage he found along the side of the road.

I was starting to get really sick by now. I had malaria. My body was swollen. I looked like a frog with a big tummy, small arms and legs, and a big head. I couldn't do anything but lie flat. All the blankets in the world couldn't keep me from getting cold. I shivered all day long. My sisters had to take turns lying on top of me to stop me from shivering to death. My family once again had to face the fact that another one of their children may die. My body had turned yellow by now, but I was a fighter and I wanted to live.

It wasn't long after my illness that we had to move to a new village in Battambang, which was supposed to be a better place. A big military truck came to move us along with about half of the village people. We took our few belongings. Pharack was still sick. His body was swollen. He had the swollen disease. We finally reached our new village to find out that the long trip on the truck was most uncomfortable for Pharack. His foot got stuck between heavy objects, and they just flattened his swollen foot.

A couple months later Pharack died. Lynn, then eight years old, was the only survivor left of her family. She was sent to work in the youth camp. We hardly ever saw her. As for me, I was too sick with one thing or another, so they said I could stay and work in the village. My mother was sent to work on building a dam and my father had to work in the rice fields from dawn to dusk. They sent my father back home a few months later.

Angka found out that my brother-in-law, Kunth, was in the military. Kunth had a friend who was a leader and really respected his hard work. Kunth begged his friend to help save his life. The friend agreed to help but wasn't sure if everything would be okay.

In the meantime, our family was scared to death. We knew that any time or at any hour Angka could come to get him. Angka usually came and took people away during the night. So when it got dark, we couldn't sleep. My father told us that if they came to get Kunth, he'd trade himself if they let Kunth go. A few days had passed and no one came. Kunth was called to his Angka friend's house and told that he'd be fine. His friend convinced the top Angka that it was a big mistake if they killed Kunth, so they agreed to let him go.

My sister Sandy delivered her third son, Reasey. He was a beautiful baby and Angka asked to adopt him, but his parents wouldn't allow that. I'd been sent away with Sandy and her husband, Kunth, and their baby to work at the rice fields far away. After a couple of months I asked Angka if I could go home to see my father, who had come back from working in the mountains. He was very ill. They told me no, but that didn't stop me. I kept asking them, and finally they agreed to let me go, but in exchange, I couldn't get any food for a whole day. I gladly exchanged it to have a chance to see my parents again.

It was dark by the time I got to my parents' village, and I went straight to their hut. I climbed up the stairs and hoped to see someone, anyone. There was my sister, Boran, sitting in the dark crying. I knew something was wrong. She wasn't supposed to be there. She was supposed to be at the labor camp. She said she had been told that our father had died, so she slipped away during work to come home. She told me what I didn't want to hear. All I could do was sit there in the dark with her and cry. We both stayed at our hut that night. We got up really early the next morning and headed to the hospital to see my mom. We found her in one of the hospital rooms, lying in bed with her face all swollen. They had already buried my father, and we weren't allowed to know where or how he was buried.

Kunth was told to move to a mountainside to cook for people who lived in that village. He was doing good with enough food to eat. He asked for permission to bring his family along, and they agreed. So Sandy, their son, and I went with him. We were there for about a month when we asked for permission to have my mom, brothers, and sisters join us. They allowed them to come, but my mom's village didn't let her come, so she gathered her four young children and packed a few things and slipped out of her village one night.

The next morning she was stopped by Angka. They told her she had to go back to the village. She was told to wait and that a truck would come and pick her up and take her back. She waited, and when Angka wasn't paying any attention, she gathered the kids and ran off and hid again. She finally got picked up by another truck that was heading to a nearby village. The whole time she and the kids lay flat in the truck so they wouldn't be seen by Angka. She later got dropped off at a road close to where me and my sister's family were staying. She stayed the night with a couple of other families that were heading in the same direction.

Our family was reunited again except for my three sisters, who were still working in the camp. We heard a rumor that my three sisters' camp was close by, so my mom and older brother Tara went to look for them one day. They had to cross water, jungle, thorns, and finally they found a place. My mom asked around, but no one seemed to know my sisters. They came back very disappointed. It was late 1978 by now.

We heard another rumor that a big fight had broken out between Pol Pot and his troops and Vietnam. Pol Pot's soldiers who lived with us started to disappear, one by one. My family decided that we needed to find my three sisters. My mom and brother said they would meet us in a couple of days whether they found them or not. They left the next morning through the same jungle, water, and thorns to the same place and asked about the children. Finally they met someone who told my mom that my sister Samach was dead. My mom cried uncontrollably but she went on searching for her other two children. While asking around, she walked past Samach to the next person and asked about her two other daughters. Samach heard my mom's voice and called out to her. They both cried and hugged each other. Later, they learned that someone else by the same name as my sister had died.

Samach knew where my sister Chharvy was but had no clue where Boran was. The last she had heard was that Boran had tried to escape and that they caught her and put her in jail. With her couple of days almost up, my mother had to return back to her other children. It was a beautiful sight when we all saw her and Tara returning with Samach and Chharvy. We had been worried sick about them.

By now, all of Angka's soldiers had disappeared. The last group of people, including my family, decided that when the sun set, we would all move out together. So, we gathered some food that Angka had left behind and waited for the sun to set. The Vietnamese troops came by and told us to stay at the big building just ahead of us.

After a couple of weeks my mom went to the market where people exchanged their jewelry for food. She had been there in the past a few times to ask about my sister, Boran. No one had heard of her. Finally, she met a lady at the market who asked if she was the one that was looking for a daughter. My mom told her, "Yes" and the lady told her she had taken in a young woman by the name of Boran. My mom was quite excited and she asked to meet with this young woman. Mom went to the lady's home and found Boran there. You can imagine the tears of joy in her eyes. We were all thrilled to see her and have our family reunited again. A month or so later we moved to Battambang. We had nothing. No place to stay, no food to eat, no clothes, no other family. Having been taken in by Kunth's family was a blessing.

❀

*SAVUTH PENN came to Minnesota in 1980 from a refugee camp in Thailand. He was sponsored by the Church World Services. In 1988 he received a bachelor of science degree in electrical engineering from Mankato State University in Minnesota. He works as an electrical engineer for an electric and gas utility company.*

❀ ❀ ❀

# The Dark Years of My Life

SAVUTH PENN

In April 1975, immediately after the New Year celebration,
my young life began to turn upside down. I was just eleven
years old. I remember overhearing my parents' conversation
that our country was at peace at last. Both of my parents
served in the military. My father was a captain. His name
was Kuhn. I believe my mother was a staff sergeant. Her name
is Sareth. They met during the police academy training for
the Royal Police and were converted to Khmer Republic
Army personnel after the coup d'état by General Lon Nol in
1970.

What my parents did not know was that their lives would
be turned upside down in a very short time. The Khmer
Rouge marched into the city of Battambang in dirty black
pajama uniforms, shoes made of used tires, and with AK–47
rifles strapped around their shoulders. They were not very
friendly. We didn't know how to react except to hang a white
flag in front of our home, as suggested by my father, as a
means of surrender and a sign of peaceful intentions.

Immediately the Khmer Rouge ordered all male military
officers and personnel to report to the school south of the
city. My mother and I buried all the military belongings
we could find in our home after we heard they would make
searches during the first week of the takeover. There were

many Khmer Rouge soldiers surrounding the school area. One day when I brought lunch for my father on my bicycle, the school was emptied. I saw people walking around looking for their husbands and fathers. When I asked them where my father was, they said the Khmer Rouge sent him to welcome our king back into the country.

One day later, the Khmer Rouge evacuated the city. My mother decided to go back to her hometown, which was about three or four miles from the city. Unfortunately, my mother received news that affected our whole family of ten forever. I had six younger sisters and one younger brother. My mother called me and one of my sisters to a quiet room and told us that my father was wounded and was being hidden in a remote location in his hometown. I started to cry and my mother said not to tell anybody, even my younger brother and sisters. My mother decided to be with my father and take care of him. She took me and my other three sisters along. The rest of the family stayed with my grandparents.

When I met my father again, about two days later, he looked so frightened and pale. He was a man who was too disciplined to show emotion or weakness but that was what I saw now. I started to cry again, and my father said not to cry but to be strong. I learned that the Khmer Rouge didn't ship my father to welcome the king. Instead, they shipped my father and the rest of the military officers to a remote area northwest of the city, near the Thai border. They asked all the officers to stand in formation and then they mass executed them, without any blindfolds, with machine guns, rifles, and grenades. Then they shot one by one at anybody who moved.

My father was buried underneath all the dead bodies. Fortunately, only one bullet went through his arm and two bullets stuck in his skull. The bullets that stuck in his skull lost momentum after passing through the other bodies. My father stayed motionless underneath the dead bodies until dark, then he tried to walk to his hometown during the night.

The whole family was shocked by this unexpected event. We thought the country was at peace at last, but instead, it was just the beginning of the dark years, years I wished that no one in the civilized world would have had to experience.

During the evacuation period Khmer society seemed to be in disarray. People tried to find their way out of the city. I tried to load the family belongings onto my bike. I could make only two trips a day between my father's hometown and my home in the city, which were about eight miles apart, because of the tremendously heavy traffic.

One month later people settled down in their chosen town, and everywhere things seemed to be very quiet, except for my family. The Khmer Rouge threatened that if anyone was hiding the enemy, the whole family would be executed. My father's relatives were very nervous. They tried to find a solution for my family. They discussed either poisoning my father, hiding him underground, or giving us an ox cart to try to get to Thailand since my father could speak Thai fluently. The first solution was too inhumane. The second solution was impossible since the rainy season was approaching and the underground cave would fill with water. The probability of getting caught if they used the third solution was high, because traveling was prohibited without a pass.

One event still haunts me even after years of trying to block it out in my subconscious. The final solution was reached by my father's brother-in-law. He informed the Khmer Rouge soldiers where my father was, and that night twelve soldiers, along with my brainwashed uncle, surrounded our cabin. They asked my mother where my father was and she told them he wasn't there. A couple soldiers climbed up with their flashlights and found him hiding in the corner of our cabin. Immediately they tied my father up and walked him about a thousand feet from our cabin.

My mother followed behind them, but they pushed her back and said she should go back and take care of the crying children.

My mother ran to my father's oldest brother, who lived nearby and also had served in the military. When he heard about the incident he ran to hide himself in the bushes close to where the Khmer Rouge soldiers were with my father. The soldiers then placed my father in the middle of the rice field, pointed flashlights at him, and shot him. My father was still standing after they fired several rounds at him. They walked toward my father and kicked him to the ground and proceeded to bayonet him.

This time, the unforgiving Khmer Rouge did not let my father survive. During the shooting I heard at least two rounds of fire which lasted only a few moments, but it seemed like forever. We stayed with our relatives for the rest of the night and waited in fright to verify if he was still alive. Unfortunately, we found his motionless body lying in the middle of the rice field. My father's bullet-ridden and bloodless body lay face up in the 90-degree heat for a whole day.

That afternoon we saw a jeep filled with the killer Khmer Rouge soldiers passing by my father's motionless and defenseless body. Apparently they had come to verify if my father was still dead. In late afternoon, under the hot and sunny sky, big black clouds suddenly started to form over the town while my father's nephews tried to bury him at the spot where he died. Suddenly, heavy rain and hail began to pour down from the sky. We felt so cold, so afraid, and so fragile without the warm and secure protection of our beloved father.

Three months later my grandpa reunited us with the rest of the family at my mother's hometown. We passed through the city, which looked like a ghost city except for a few demon Khmer Rouge soldiers riding their bicycles, laughing and smiling at one another. I tried to keep my anger and hatred from showing. We were even afraid to look at them.

We were afraid they might detect what we knew about their unjustifiable actions against their own innocent Khmer people.

For the next three years my family went through many events that I will never be able to forget. According to the uncivilized and insane Khmer Rouge government, Khmer society was classified as consisting of two types: the old and the new people. The people who they liberated before April 1975 they called the old people, and they provided them with better treatment and living conditions. The people who they liberated after April 1975 they called the new people, whom they treated as their slaves to do all the labor–intensive work without adequate food, supplies, and housing. My family was in the latter group. My mother was forced to remarry, and if she refused, they threatened to terminate her life. Because of my mother's background with the Khmer Republic Army, which they considered to be their number one enemy, she had no choice but to accept the arrangement. My new stepfather and my mother had a son about a year later.

In the meantime, I was sent to a remote farming area with a group of other young boys to build an irrigation system for increasing the rice production. My older sister was sent to another area with a group of young girls. Two of my sisters died from starvation and disease. My mother had to escape to another, safer area, called Zone 3, with my new half–brother, since the Khmer Rouge was looking for her.

My dispersed family members lived under constant fear and hunger. We were too hungry to show any sign of hatred or revenge. Every night seemed to last forever. It was hard to fall asleep with an empty stomach. Sometimes I filled my stomach with water in order to feel full so I could sleep easier. As it turned out, I had to get up more frequently to relieve myself. I remember that the other boys and I extended a long tube from the floor to the nearest outside bush to relieve ourselves during the night. Unfortunately,

❀
47

our Khmer Rouge master destroyed our energy-saving device the next morning.

During the day I would hunt for food like snakes and rats or anything that moved. This was allowed only during a short break after the long labor-intensive work. My body was so thin and weak from lack of adequate nutrition. The other young boys were in the same condition as me. We looked like grandpas to one another. We rarely played or had long conversations because we lacked energy and tried to conserve it for the next day's work quota.

During the last year under the Khmer Rouge's rule, my sisters and brother and I joined my mother in Zone 3. While at Zone 3 I was sent to clear new land for growing cotton. There was plenty of food to eat and a lot of tropical fruits to pick. It was the first time that I felt life was worth living, but I was so sad that I never had a chance to see my family as frequently as I liked to. It seemed that the whole country was divided into many zones. Each zone had its own leadership but was under one insane and merciless Khmer Rouge government. Some zones, such as Zone 3, had better treatment and more mercy than other zones.

In late 1978 and early 1979 the Vietnamese invaded Cambodia, driving the Khmer Rouge government into the jungle in western Cambodia. Without any more Khmer Rouge masters around, my family, immediate relatives, and other people returned to the city to their original homes. Except for cement columns, my home was no longer standing. Our family and some of my immediate relatives stayed in other people's homes. When we did a head count of our family, two were missing and four were dead.

For those four years of living under the inhumane treatment of an insane Khmer Rouge government, every day seemed like months, months seemed like years, and years seemed like centuries. Time seemed to be at a standstill. There was no schooling and no prospect for the future. The only things I learned were hatred and revenge for my father and sisters' deaths. Even after seventeen years, I'm not so sure I can say the word *forgive*, but I surely will never forget what the Khmer Rouge did to my family and their own Khmer people. I hope such an insane government will never rule Cambodia or any civilized country again.

*CHARLES OK (pictured with his family) fled Cambodia in 1982 for the Khao-I-Dang refugee camp in Thailand because he was being starved and harassed by the Vietnamese. He married in 1984 and came to the United States in 1985 under the sponsorship of a Catholic agency. He currently works as a mail carrier.*

# Jail Without Walls

**CHARLES OK**

**H**ave you ever been hungry, tortured, suffering, losing hope in life, waiting your turn to be killed? Have you ever thought that your life was less valuable than a piece of bread, a piece of paper, or a piece of candy? This phenomenon happened to the Cambodian people under the genocidal regime ruled by Pol Pot, Ieng Sary, and Khieu Samphan.

My former name was Satya Ok. I was born in 1958. My family lived in Phnom Penh. On April 17, Cambodian people celebrate the New Year. But on this day in 1975, instead of celebrating, all the city people were forced to the countryside by the revolutionary army. This was after the Khmer Rouge had taken control of all the cities in Cambodia. They told my family and others that after three days, we could return home. They said, "This season we evacuate you because we are afraid that the city will be bombed by America."

My family lived near the Interior Department, on the east side of the city. Everyone was driven out of the city. About three to four miles away, along the road, people put up tents on the side of someone's house or near the temples. My family was very lucky because my mother had a cousin who lived near Wat Champa. We lived with them for a while. Three days, three weeks, and then three months passed, and we were still waiting to go back home, like a drought that waits for the rain. Food was getting short. Money became useless, and only gold and silver were traded for food. Some people couldn't handle this kind of suffering and depression, and they committed suicide.

The city now looked like a ghost town. There were only Khmer Rouge soldiers. These soldiers registered people who wanted to go back to their city jobs. Many registered. But, instead of being allowed to return to their jobs, some were killed. Others were sent to Pursat and Battambang in western Cambodia to work in forced labor camps.

After staying with my mother's cousin for a while, we decided to move to the east side of the Mekong River. While there we were forced to live in a group and work in a cooperative. The amount of food we received depended on how many family members there were and how much work each of them could perform. There was never enough food.

Early in 1976, it was harvest time. The chairman of the cooperative asked people to register to go to Battambang or Pursat. They told us that there was much rice left in those fields because there were not enough people to do the harvesting. Since we'd left our home, we never had had enough food to eat. Because Pursat and Battambang were provinces full of rice, we decided to go without hesitation. We boarded a train and got off at Pursat.

Each member of the family was separated to work and live with their own age group. I was put into the teenager group. Clothes that had color were prohibited. Only black

clothes were worn. Black shoes were made from tires of trucks
or cars. There was no makeup, no high heels, no boots, no
jewelry.

Every day and night we prayed and thought only about
food. Day by day, all of us looked more haggard. Whenever
we had a break we gathered and talked about nothing but
food, food, and food. Because we were so hungry we had to
eat anything we could. Sometimes people died after eating
the wrong food. Because we had eating disorders, we became sick. The common diseases were diarrhea, malaria, and
dysentery.

Modern medicine was banned by the Khmer Rouge. Each
of us was forced to use traditional medicine to cure all kinds
of diseases. I was the first one in my family to get sick. Luckily, my mom was able to smuggle some modern medicine
from a friend. Later my mom got sick. My brother and I had
nothing left to trade for modern medicine to help her. A
couple of weeks later, my mom died.

I was working so hard to survive. I was sent from my
teenage cooperative to a district camp, then to a regional
camp. The rations they provided me were much better than
for those who lived in the cooperative or district groups. Yet
it was still not enough. Food, salt, and tobacco were plentiful
in the warehouse. But the revolutionary people didn't want
to give us the food. Everyone became a burglar, and if we
were caught, death was certain.

I lived far from where my brother lived. Sometimes I had
permission to visit him. One day when I did visit they asked
me to help bury bodies because they didn't have enough
people to help. There were thousands of dead people everywhere. In the winter most of the land was wet and full of
water. Because there were so many bodies, they buried one
body on top of the other. In the winter they couldn't dig
deep because water would come out of the ground. When a

corpse was swollen it was hard to bury, making it easy for foxes and other animals to dig for it at night.

It was a scary time for whoever was still alive. Besides starving to death, we were confronted with another kind of massacre. Every night and day young adults, most of them men, were tied up to be killed. The army said that these people were either former soldiers, former police officers, CIA agents or KGB members. They were the enemy of the revolution. "We must clean up these people." They were guilty before proven guilty. Some knew that they were going to be killed, so they escaped to the jungle but were caught and killed as an example and warning to others who tried to run away. Some committed suicide. Day by day the villages grew more empty except for widows.

The relationship between the Khmer Rouge and Communist Vietnam was once very close. It was said, "Vietnam is the brother and Cambodia is the sister. We are like lips and teeth." But this relationship became sour and bitter. Finally they started to fight each other. Because of the fighting in the co-op and district areas, the Khmer Rouge searched for whoever had Vietnamese blood and killed them. A lot of these people, along with former soldiers and police officers who had been caught, were sent to learning centers to be killed.

People who lived near the Vietnam border were now being evacuated. They were sent to Battambang and Pursat. They were killed, including whole families, babies and adults. The Khmer Rouge accused these people of spying for Vietnam.

One day I was sent to another camp to clear the jungle. I had to travel through the village where my brother lived. When I met him, he was very skinny. He and I cried and cried. I gave him half of my food and I still remember the words he said to me: "Dear brother, the food that you just gave me is like a ton of gold or a big party that I never had in my life." A few months later, I tried to visit him again. Unfortunately, he had passed away. Since then I have become a lonely person. Sometimes I sit down and cry and think about the past. But life goes on, and I have to learn to take care of myself.

MOLY LY *came to the United States in 1980 with his only surviving sister in Cambodia, Kuy Ny Ly, through the USCC from the Red Cross Refugee Camp in Thailand. He was sponsored by his sister in the United States, Nay Ky Ly. He now lives in Santa Ana, California, where he works for the U.S. Postal Service. While working there full time he attended California State University at Fullerton part time. He obtained a bachelor's degree in computer science in August 1995. In June 1996 Moly married a Khmer woman whom he met while visiting Cambodia.*

❀  ❀  ❀

# *Witnessing the Horror*

### MOLY LY

It was the morning of April 17, 1975. The gleaming sun rose gradually, emerging from the horizon in a captivating view. In contrast, our lives little by little began to move into darkness. Although I was young at the time, I learned a lot from my brother Eng Ly, a journalist. He inspired me. He taught me how disastrous it was going to be under this new regime. Knowing the Communist theory and its indiscriminate manslaughter, I was wondering, at the young age of thirteen if we would be fortunate enough to see the sunlight again. Things I used to do in life, a modest but happy and rustic life, seemingly would vanish in this obscure and unknown world of darkness.

That day we found ourselves hiding inside the house pretending to be unaware of any outside events. But soon we were awakened by a throng of Khmer Rouge soldiers banging on our front door. "Go or we will shoot!" screamed one of them. We could no longer pretend. Grasping all our belongings, my mother, my sisters Naykea, Navy, and Kuyny, two brothers-in-law, two nieces, and two nephews left Phnom Penh with thousands of other families. We walked with our bundles on our shoulders and heads.

Understanding what the Communists would do to him, my brother Eng departed a different way from our family in an attempt to escape northward to Thailand. He was close to six feet tall, the opposite of me, and a well-known journalist, so he was very hard to conceal. For him the victory of the Khmer Rouge was fraught with danger. We could only pray for him and wish him the best of luck.

A group of Khmer Rouge soldiers threatened the crowds, "Go! Go! Hurry! Hurry!" They were dressed in black with red kramas wrapped around their heads and rifles slung on their shoulders. I started to hear small children cry, and I cried too. We were heading to Takeo, the province in which my mother and father were born and raised. On the way there corpses were lying everywhere. At every stop we made we needed to find water to cook with or to drink.

At the first stop I carried my water bucket to the nearby river. About forty-five feet away from me was a dead body floating and swelling up like a dead buffalo in the water. I had no choice but to boil the water, drink it, and cook with it. I cried at night with hopelessness and despair. I knew that this was just the beginning of the long journey. I asked myself why any human being had to suffer like this.

We arrived at Takeo at last, but after a few months we were dispatched to a small village in Battambang Province. My oldest sister, Naykea, and her family were sent in a different direction since she and her husband were former teachers. In our village there were about 300 families. Each family owned a hut that was about twelve feet long by twelve feet wide. People were divided up into five classes: small children, bigger children, single women and men, married women and men, and elderly women and men.

Each class was forced to work in a different field. Everyone had to endure hard work from dawn to dusk. They got a few hours of rest if they worked close to the village. If you worked far from the village you only got half an hour to one hour of rest and mealtime. Being fourteen at the time, I was first put into the single men class but then was sent back to the bigger children group because I was a little too small. On and off, my sister Kuyny and I were sent to work far from the village. We were called *kong chalat*, meaning mobile troops.

Our duties included building dikes, digging canals, liquidating the forest by removing roots, chopping logs and branches, and setting old brush on fire. We mixed up human remains with soil. The heavy buckets carrying the soil were attached to a flat stick that dug into our shoulders. Every day we were starving yet forced to work harder. Small children who could walk and work (as young as five or six years old) were given jobs. Our sustenance was a small amount of watery rice.

Our lives were gradually being claimed by these ferocious animals, the illiterate and brainwashed Khmer Rouge, whose leaders were obedient to China. Some people were accused of being lazy and were taken out and brutally executed simply because they became mentally sick or were physically unable to work. Teachers, lawyers, doctors, former soldiers—especially high-ranking officers—and other intellectuals were the most vulnerable and were targeted for execution. Some were lucky and hid their real identities. But many were often wrongly accused because of the way they looked. Wearing eyeglasses (remains from the old regime) could mean death because the Khmer Rouge thought that glasses meant the person was educated. The Khmer Rouge said that a firing squad was a waste of bullets. Instead of bullets, the Khmer Rouge killed by beating people with the back of a hoe. They called this *vay choul*.

Being hungry for one day is hard enough. But, day after day, month after month, and year after year, hunger debilitated us to the point of insanity. We cooked and ate nonpoi-

sonous grass like it was a vegetable, just to gratify our hungry stomachs. The swarming insects that were edible became
nourishment. What had once been repulsive foods became
desirable. Some people were so hungry that they dug up
dead bodies and slit the flesh and fried it. One man was
caught doing this and was put to death.

My little niece Viphea was about two years old. The only
words she knew how to speak were, *buy*, *Pa*, and *Mak*, which
meant in English, "steamed rice," "Dad," and "Mom." She kept
repeating these three words. Her father, with his swollen feet,
hands, and face, could not stand to hear his wailing, holler-
ing little daughter. He started to slap her around. There was
no question in my mind that my brother-in-law Ngeth was
abnormally susceptible to the agony of starvation. A former
high school math teacher before the fall of the country and
considered by many to be a gentleman, he now couldn't
differentiate between right and wrong. My sister Navy
stopped the beating and separated the two. She also looked
very pale with the same disease as her husband, a swollen
face, feet, and hands. This disease was the most prevalent.
Malaria and dysentery were also epidemics and claimed
many lives.

I wasn't even sure I could rally my energy to stay alive. I
had excruciating pain. I no longer cried but accepted this
horrifying experience as if it were normal. Nightfall meant
heaven to us. When I went to sleep on my bed made from
twigs, I wished that I could close my eyes and never wake up
to see the sun again.

After a few months my little niece became swollen, like
an overinflated water balloon. She was so weak. She seldom
pleaded for steamed rice. She either lost her memory or was
too ill to talk. When she did speak, it was no longer to say
Pa or Mak, but only buy. I had never seen her smile. Her
gloomy appearance begged for compassion. She never had a
chance to understand the meaning of joy. Nothing on earth

could have tormented me more than to witness a little girl come out of her mother's womb only to be tortured slowly, day in and day out.

One early morning my sister Navy ran feebly but hastily outside and around the hut. With her little daughter in her arms, she screamed for help. Her unusual strength indicated that something unusual was happening. Viphea's eyes looked so spiritless. Her pupils rolled reluctantly up and down. She was unable to speak. My sister's tears were flowing from her pale, swollen eyes. Over and over again Navy begged, screamed, and cried as she scurried around the hut. Our neighbors could only leap from their shacks and stare at Viphea with wide eyes filled with sorrow. About an hour later Viphea died. Although we were filled with intense grief, there were no regrets for her death, because the price of staying alive was too high. I knew she was at peace and I prayed for her.

Some time later my brother-in-law Ngeth was escorted out of the village. We were told that they sent him to the hospital because he was too sick to work. I became suspicious, and then I realized that he would be gone forever. We were powerless to help him. Three people that day, including Ngeth, were taken away by the Khmer Rouge. They were all former high school teachers and we assumed they were murdered. They never came back.

About fifty families were transferred to another district. The Khmer Rouge put these unfortunate families in a big American military truck and took them away. A few days later it was revealed by the local soldiers that these families had Vietnamese blood and for that reason were put to death. I lost quite a few friends, most of them were Chinese Cambodians. The complexion of their skin was only a little lighter than mine.

After learning that Navy was a midwife, the Khmer Rouge used her to train their comrades who couldn't read. After teaching them what she knew she was expelled from the training. A few months later she grew very sick and was put into the hospital near the village. The hospital had no doctors and no nurses, only a group of illiterate comrades who were trained for a few months like the ones my sister had trained. She was better off staying in this hospital than staying at home and subjecting herself to harassment for being unable to work.

Since Navy was at one time helpful to the Khmer Rouge and because she was so sick, I was allowed to stay with her. Navy's whole body was swollen terribly. She later died in my arms. It was devastating to me since I was vigilant over her for a couple of days, knowing that she didn't have long to live. Speaking incoherently in a grief-stricken voice, I cried bitterly and emotionally. Navy's dead body was buried with two other dead bodies. My request to place her underground in her own grave was rejected.

After Navy's death I went back home to be with my mother, who had the same disease as Navy. I was almost beaten to death with a long stick just because I disobeyed the order not to collect any remaining potatoes after Angka finished gathering them. I was trying to help feed my mother. My black shirt was saturated with blood from my back. My mother wept. The next day I could hardly move and was incapable of going to work. Because I tried to help my mother I was deprived of rice water. It was a nightmare to see my ill mother carrying buckets of water from a stagnant pond to take care of me. I should have been taking care of her. She was in her mid-fifties but looked like she was in her mid-seventies. Her weak and swollen body had to endure so much to save herself and her son.

Months later I was sent to work far from my mother in one of the kong chalat. My sister Kuyny was almost always in a mobile troop because she was in the single-women class. Although I begged not to go because my mother was too sick to stay alone, I was refused. My mother was then sent to the same hospital where my sister died. About a month later, while I was working, the bad news came to me. A village leader who happened to be there said that my mother had just passed away. I asked to go see my mother's body, but the Khmer Rouge didn't let me. "She's dead. What good is it to see her?" Even before my mother's death, when I asked to visit her, they said, "You're not a doctor. What good is it to see her?" I was no longer scared of dying, and I ran away from the work camp to the hospital, knowing that I would face serious consequences if I got caught. At the hospital I learned that my mother was already buried with one other dead person.

Before long I heard the news from my aunt that my oldest sister Naykea, her husband, Try, and one surviving child had come to look for us. They found only the empty hut. Her family had been allowed to leave their town because of a disastrous flood. She found a village to live in about five miles from our village. I never thought I would see her again because she and her husband were former schoolteachers.

I sneaked away again from my village, this time to search for my oldest sister. I was a worn-out, skeletal figure craving food. I knew beyond a doubt that I was running out of time. But my determination to live remained inside me. On the way I decided to go over to the rice field and gather rice in its husk and consume it as fast as I possibly could to fill up my stomach. I got caught by the kong chloup, who were Khmer Rouge spies. This time I knew I was in big trouble. It was getting dark, and I was dragged into a jail.

Once there, I was stunned to see only four women and a man. Without observing the clothes they wore, it was difficult to tell the difference between the man and the women. They had extremely fragile figures. Bones were popping out from everywhere in their bodies. At night our feet were cuffed with a special kind of wood to prevent us from escaping. At dawn we were dragged to work near the jail, plucking the soil.

The next day, one of the women died in her sleep. Her ankles had been cuffed. I now realized that this was a death camp to cruelly torture people by starving and overworking them. Sometimes they threw food scraps at our faces and laughed. Other times we were beaten for being so exhausted from the hard work. I could no longer function like a human being. I knew in my heart that my spirit was going to die.

The door to the jail was opened as usual the next morning. It was time to go to work. A dark-complexioned man with a friendly smile said to me, "Come with me. Your sister is waiting for you." I breathed a sigh of relief. Naykea had heard from a friend that I was a prisoner, so she implored this generous man, who was a village leader, to help me. He was a remarkable, warmhearted man, even though he was trusted by the Khmer Rouge. In this new village our lives were better. But we were still very skinny and sick looking.

A few months later the Vietnamese came and chased the Khmer Rouge away, but tragically, Naykea had the disease of swollen face, hands, and feet. My sister was excited about the invasion, knowing that no other regime could be worse than the Khmer Rouge, but she was fighting for her life. Everyone left the village but us because Naykea couldn't walk. Finally, Naykea died. Her death was so regrettable and frustrating.

The sinister menace of Communism not only destroyed my family but also caused the death of millions of Cambodians. The effects of the Khmer Rouge's hatred and massacre of its own people will never fade away. Hitler is dead, but Pol Pot and his entourage are still alive and craving a return. Why do we as human beings condone such a notorious, rep-

rehensible phenomenon by allowing these ferocious murderers to still be loose?

I dedicate this story to my beloved mother, grandmother,
brother, sisters, brother-in-law, niece, and nephews, who left
this world in agony during the years of horror.

*SAROM PRAK lived at the Sungai Besi refugee camp in Malaysia for seven years. While at the camp, he was a leader of the small group of Cambodians sharing with camp officials and nongovernmental organizations the ongoing plight the remaining Cambodian refugees face. He recently left the camp with his brother after New Zealand approved Sarom's immigration papers. Sarom and his brother were reunited in New Zealand with their grandmother, their only surviving relative besides an aunt, who lives in Idaho.*

---

❀   ❀   ❀

# The Unfortunate Cambodia

### SAROM PRAK

Under a light of a candle in my unit in Sungai Besi Camp
in Malaysia, at 2 A.M., I am sitting alone thinking about my
life in the past and in the future. I have been living in this
detention camp for seven years without any resolution. I ask
myself, Why am I alone? Who or what made me be alone
like this? This is a very complicated question that I try to
explain to everyone I know, particularly Cambodian people,
so that they don't forget why.

From 1975 to 1979, I was a slave in the Pol Pot regime. The
whole country was annihilated by the Khmer Rouge during
their years in power. When I recall the brutal massacre of
millions of innocent people, I am dreadfully terrified.

After the Khmer Rouge takeover in April 1975 in Cambodia, at least 2 million people were driven into the countryside. Men, women, and children were banished from the
cities by Khmer Rouge soldiers. Angka divided us into city
people, whom they called "new," and country people, who
were called "old." This was the first time I had heard of the
Khmer Rouge. During the leadership of the Khmer Rouge all
of Cambodia was put into vast forced labor camps. Most
temples were destroyed, and many monks and nuns were
killed. They broke the sentiment between wives, husbands,
and children. They segregated them into separate work

groups, and everyone had to eat in communal dining halls near where they worked. We were not allowed to see each other. If we wanted to meet our parents or relatives we had to escape from the camp secretly. We were chastised seriously if the Khmer Rouge got word of this.

I was in a camp in Takeo province. All of us were awakened at 6 A.M., and we labored until our first meal, at 11:30 A.M. The Khmer Rouge permitted us to eat one can of rice mixed with the skins of potatoes. This fed 200 persons. After that we continued working again from 1:30 to 6 P.M. Then we were again fed a meal. At night we labored from 7:30 to midnight. If one of us pretended to be ill he was allowed to eat only a bit of gruel. If he was always sick, he would disappear. When his relatives would ask where he was, the Khmer Rouge would reply rudely that he'd been sent to Angka. No one came back when the Khmer Rouge sent someone to Angka. Lamentably, all of us were coerced to labor without stopping in the rain and under the hot sun. During this time there were many kinds of work, including digging a trench and canal, making a dam, and so on. We were the Cambodian slave labor.

In this Communist regime nobody could marry without approval from Angka. Men were not able to propose to any girls. Angka compelled some people to marry even though they had never seen each other before. Angka prepared a wedding party for 70 to 100 couples every now and then in Takeo. The forced marriages were a good way for some of the people who had power—like the soldiers, the chiefs of villages and districts—to molest young girls until they got pregnant. Many of these girls were forced to marry these men, and sometimes they were killed because of being afraid to marry them. Flirtations, adultery, and love affairs were reasons for execution. No one could complain or argue with them. If someone dared to do this, he or she would disappear.

The Communists practiced killing several million innocent people. The young Khmer Rouge soldiers not only butchered strangers but also their own parents. The principles of Angka implanted this idea into the minds of the soldiers: "We were born by virtue of the sexual passion of the parents, so we don't respect them. If the parents do something wrong, we must kill them."

The Khmer Rouge killed many of the new people after telling them to load up the salt from some province or another. They gathered the people together, took them to an isolated spot, and killed them. The people had thought they were going somewhere to work, but none came back.

"When I went into the jungle near the hamlet to look for wood for the communal dining halls, I saw many bones and dead bodies," said a villager. At another location in the district were more bodies. This is where my father was killed. My father was a captain in the army from the time Cambodia was a French colony. The Khmer Rouge accused him of being a CIA agent for America. Then they executed him.

At that time I lived in a pagoda in Takeo. About 100 meters to the east of the pagoda I saw dead bodies appearing from the pits because wolves ate them at night.

Before they were butchered, some innocent people were coerced to dig small pits for themselves. None of us had the energy to fight back because we didn't have enough food to eat. After the new pit was ready, the young soldiers tied the arms of their victims and ordered them to kneel near the edge of the pits. Then the young soldiers began to hit them with heavy hoes, thick bamboo sticks, or axes.

During the killings there were shouts of pain and moaning. Blood ran from their nostrils, ears, and mouths as the objects crushed the backs of their heads. Some victims were not yet dead when the soldiers pushed earth over them. Throughout the country, large pits had been dug by the laborers. Then trucks carried the blindfolded prisoners to be dragged to the edge of the pits. One by one the prisoners fell into the pits after being hit.

The Khmer Rouge killed teenagers. They held their arms up, disemboweled them, and cut out their livers and gall bladder and put them into sacks. Some of the Khmer Rouge soldiers ate the livers of their victims. The young boys moaned and shouted out in pain. They disfigured the bodies and slashed the throats of young children and babies. The Khmer Rouge tore the babies into pieces.

Some people who accidentally broke the knives, hoes, axes, and plows they were working with were slaughtered by the Khmer Rouge. Generators were used to electrocute some men. Others were beheaded with machetes. The Khmer Rouge used pincers to cut off the nipples of women, and they took their fingernails out. In some places they forced people to take off their clothing. The Khmer Rouge collected the clothing to distribute to people and said that the clothing was a present from Angka. Some people recognized their relatives' clothes, but none dared to say so or to ask any questions about them.

❀
70

In 1977, I moved from the 105th district to the 109th district in Tram Kak district, Takeo Province, with the other people. In this area there was a killing center to the east of the hamlet at the rice field. When the executors slaughtered people, they generally switched on a blaring loudspeaker because they didn't want the villagers to hear the shouts of pain and moaning. After a while, when the villagers heard the loudspeaker they knew that the Khmer Rouge were slaying people. So the villagers who lived around a killing center wept bitter tears quietly.

Every nook and cranny was demolished by the Communist Khmer Rouge. During this time, there were no planes, no train service, no mail. There was nothing.

I am a survivor of the Communist regime. I have undergone bitter suffering for many years in Cambodia. So I take every opportunity to notify others and insist that people in all four corners of the earth fully realize what happens when people slay other human beings. I am not you and you are not me, but we are all human beings. Life is not something to sell.

ROEUN SAM escaped to the Thai border in 1979 to find food and shelter in order to help her starving family also escape. Roeun's mother,
father, and two younger sisters followed her to the border camp. The
Sams were under siege in the camp for several months, until the Red
Cross took them to Khao-I-Dang camp in Thailand. Roeun was not sponsored but applied to come to the United States. After transfers to several
more camps, Roeun, her parents, and one sister arrived in the United
States on March 29, 1983. Roeun now is reunited with three sisters and
a brother, who all live in the States. She has one sister remaining in
Cambodia. Another sister was killed during the Khmer Rouge assault in
1975. She still cares for her parents, and she is married and has a daughter, Darazyl. Roeun is the Cambodian interpreter for a clinic of the largest
health department in the state of Washington. She is working toward a
degree in counseling and co-leads groups for Cambodian trauma survivors and for Cambodian chemical dependency groups.

❀  ❀  ❀

# *Living in the Darkness*

## ROEUN SAM

I can never forget the Khmer Rouge Communist regime. When I was fourteen years old the country collapsed and the Khmer Rouge forced people to leave town. We had to go to the jungle at gunpoint. The Khmer Rouge were telling us that we had to leave only for three days because the United States was going to drop a bomb. They said they would clear out the town until the enemy was gone. They told us not to bring any belongings except for a few, for we would be back in three days.

Our family didn't take much. We didn't prepare. My father was very old and said not to bring very many things. The Khmer Rouge went straight to our family. "Leave now. If you don't leave, we are going to shoot you!" I ran to pick up my books so that when I came back I would be prepared for school. I went and said good-bye to my coconut tree and mango tree and then to my house, the place that brought me fun and joy. Then I cried. My father was standing there looking at me, and he said sadly, "Don't worry. We are coming back. You will not lose your tree."

We walked about twenty kilometers on the dusty, dry road, and the Khmer Rouge, dressed in black, walked behind us with guns pointed. Their shoes were made of tire rubber, and they wore red and white striped scarves. They harassed and humiliated us. They said that I was stupid because I was riding my bike and carrying my chemistry and history books, along with a book that had been a gift from my teacher. "Who is going to come back and study?" They laughed in a sinister way. Then one of them told me to give them my books so they could tear a page in which to roll a cigarette. I had sisters and I was afraid they would hurt them, so I didn't say anything and gave them the books. They tore up my books and then began to smoke.

The Khmer Rouge leader, Me Kong, put our family into a place they used to store rice seed. At this time we had eight in our family, and we never saw the sun unless we were sent outside. It was a place with no windows and a very small door. It was made of wood and bamboo. Cow dung was used to paint the dwelling. Inside were many scorpions and spiders. They fell from the ceiling, biting my family. The place smelled, especially when it rained. After a while we were all told to go to work in different places. Our family was broken up.

They put me with others my age and had me work in the field to watch the cows. Every day I watched the cows, and after I fed them at night I went to the place where the children laid on the ground to sleep. We didn't have a roof, wall, or bed. We slept on the ground. I worked so hard and got so little to eat. We only ate one meal a day, at lunch. Angka measured each serving, only about a cup and a half, which was mostly broth and maybe two tablespoons of rice. They also gave us a small piece of salt to suck on as we ate. Sometimes we didn't even get salt. We fought each other for it.

One day as I was watching the cows eat grass, I noticed that a few of my cows were missing. I smelled something like a dead animal. My cows were running toward the smell, and I followed them. By the time I got there the cows were licking the dead body's clothes. Some were standing there sniffing. It was a human body that had just been killed. You could see her long black hair and the string around her hands. I looked around and saw people who had been shot and their heads were smashed in. There were at least one hundred people dead. This was the place they took people to kill. I was very scared because if I couldn't get the cows back, I would be killed or punished. I whistled for the cows to come and we hurried back.

I saw so many of the prisoners they took to kill. The prisoners were blindfolded, and their hands were tied behind their backs. I thought they had done something wrong. I didn't realize until I had been moved to a different place what really was happening.

One place I remember clearly is Thunder Hill. One day at this camp they called all the kids to come to a meeting. We had to walk in a line across ponds and creeks. Our clothes got wet, but it didn't matter because we were used to it. We had to go single file because Angka was afraid we would escape.

On the way I saw my two younger sisters. They were in different camps than I and were also being forced to go to the meeting. I saw my youngest sister from very far away and we tried to look at each other. I couldn't ask her how she was doing; we only stood and stared at each other. We weren't supposed to get out of line and had to look straight ahead. I tried to recognize their walk. Both of them were so skinny and didn't have good pants to wear. My younger sister wanted to cry when she saw me, but crying was forbidden by Angka. I turned away from my sisters so the Khmer Rouge wouldn't see her cry and discover that we were sisters.

The meeting took place at the temple. They had all of us sit in line. The children sat in front. We looked like grandmothers and grandfathers, we were so thin. We were too tired to smile, laugh, or cry. We were so dry that we had no tears left.

The meeting started. They called the two prisoners. "If someone betrays Angka, they will be executed. We want everyone to know that these people are bad examples, and we don't want other people to be like this." Two of them walked the prisoners to the middle, which was in front of us. Angka talked with a microphone. He told us to come to the front so we could see those who had betrayed Angka. They deserved this. All the kids like me were forced by the leader to sit in front to see one of the prisoners. Angka said, "If anyone cries or shows empathy or compassion for this person, they will be punished by receiving the same treatment."

Angka told someone to get the prisoner on his knees. The prisoner had to confess what he had done wrong. Then the prisoner began to talk but he didn't confess anything. Instead, he screamed, "God, I did not do anything wrong. Why are they doing this to me? I work day and night, never complain, and even though I get sick and I have a hard time getting around, I satisfy you so you won't kill people. I never thought to betray Angka. This is injustice. I have done nothing wrong! Arthmel Atsasna." In Cambodian this means that Communists destroy their own people, culture, religion and, ancestors. "You kill people without reason. This is injustice!"

Suddenly one of them hit him from the back, pushed him, and he fell face to the ground. It was raining. We sat in the rain, and then the rain became blood. He was hit with a shovel and then he went unconscious and began to have a seizure. Then Angka took out a sharp knife and cut the man from his breastbone all the way down to his stomach. They took out his organs.

When I saw this I felt so shocked, like I was blind. It felt like they were hitting me just as they hit the prisoner. The person that cut him open took a sharp piece of wire and stuck it in what I think was the liver and bowels. They tied the organs with wire on the handlebars of a bicycle and biked away, leaving a bloody trail.

Angka calmly told us over the microphone, "All girls and boys, you have seen with your own eyes. If someone feels compassion or sympathy for the enemy that has just died, then you will be punished just like him." My spirit and mind were gone somewhere already. I know I saw them carry the bloody organs away. Now I wondered if this was true, did it happen? I was now a prisoner in my mind and my body.

My mind says, Don't remember, because this could be me. The air smelled like blood. Clear rain drops coming from the sky became blood. I was enraged and shaky this first time I saw a killing. I said to myself, "Oh, my God." My mind shut down. My eyes didn't even blink. Then Angka told us to get in line, and we all headed back to the place we lived.

When we returned Angka called all of us for another meeting before we were allowed to eat. I felt very sorrowful, angry, and hurt that I couldn't help this person who died unjustly. They told us to be strong. They brainwashed us into not following the dead prisoner's path, to continue to work like thunder.

That night I couldn't sleep. I remembered the face of the prisoner, his words, and what they had done to him. It was cruel and inhumane. I was so angry inside. I couldn't forgive them for what they did to their own people. At 3:30 A.M. I hadn't fallen asleep yet, and then the whistle blew. I had to get up and get in line.

I was at so many camps, and again they moved me. Here my job was to fix the small dams that supplied water to the rice fields. If there was too much water the rice would spoil and die. If this happened we would be punished and not get any rice. Sometimes I had to dig in the small creek in order to get clay for the dam. I was very small, and I had to swim to get the clay out of the creek bed. I then had to swim with the clay to where the dam was.

The water was full of leeches. I was afraid of the leeches and had trouble doing my job. Angka told me to be fast and work hard. If I didn't, they were going to send me to some place from which I'd never come back. "We will send you to eat dirt or eat the shovel we use to hit people with. You'll die." So sometimes I just let the leeches stay on me. When they are filled with blood they fall off.

When night came I always worried. I stayed up even when they told us to go to sleep. Angka walked around with a flashlight at night to see who was asleep and who wasn't. I was afraid that maybe next time it would be me. I would die before I saw the sun rise. I had little rest, and then I heard the whistle and inside I sighed, "Oh, I'm alive!" I got up and got in line. From one night to the next it was the same. On a clear night I could see the stars and the moon and would feel a little better. I always prayed, "God, please don't let the sun go down."

A doghouse was better than where we were staying. Bushes were our walls. We slept on rice hay. Thick bags made of hemp that held rice seed were our blankets. The bags smelled, and mine was completely stained and falling apart. We could never wash them or they'd be ruined. Then what would I have to cover up with? At night I would crawl into it and curl up. It would keep me from being scared and cold. I wasn't cold from the weather but because I was alone. I felt cold inside.

Every night I could hear the footsteps of Khmer Rouge soldiers walking around. They were laughing and drinking, and they enjoyed killing. They took the kids to kill. I saw them. They walked them outside and said, "We want you to join your family." The kids were so happy and said good-bye to us. "I am going to see my parents. See, Angka is very good!" I would peek my head out of my bag and see them go. They never came back.

I was starving. One night I ate very small snails and the shells. After the soldiers went to sleep I sneaked out to their fire and used a broken pan to fry the snails a little. My stomach was crawling back and forth, and I had to eat. I shared the snails with my friend. Afterwards I got into my bag and ate more. A rat came in and ate my toenail. I slept so heavy I didn't even know. My blanket protected me. Later on someone stole my blanket, and then I had nothing.

Another time I saw a forest duck and knew there would

be eggs where the duck was. The sun was setting. I jumped into the water after the duck. I lost the duck, who was faster than me because I was so weak and skinny. The water was chest high. I thought maybe there were eggs in there. I found one! It was lying in the middle of a human skull. I picked it up and took the egg out and searched and found three more eggs. One egg was stuck close to the mouthful of teeth. I thought that the dead person wanted to eat this egg. I took it, then I put it back. I told the dead body, "Don't let me see you in my mind." I put the skull and the egg on the bank of the pond. I tried to find more eggs. I felt the bottom of the pond and it felt like pieces of wood. Whenever I reached down to pick something up, I would get a handful of white bones. Later, I went to a pond that was used for bathing and pretended to be bathing so that I could eat my eggs.

I was sent to another place where I continued to build dams. We each had to dig one meter of dirt across and one meter deep every day. Then we had to carry the dirt up a slippery ladder. One day I was walking in line to go home after work with my best friend, who was behind me. I would turn and look to make sure she was there. Once in a while she would whisper to me. We had been given a potato each! I was saving mine to give to my mother and father if Angka allowed me to see them. My friend was saving hers for her nieces and nephews. After we got to the village they gave us each a white cloth to wrap around our bodies like a blanket. Our clothes were torn apart.

One night Angka cooked us delicious chicken soup. At that moment I thought that Angka wasn't so bad. Maybe we have a new Angka! My friend didn't eat that much because she saw the Khmer Rouge soldiers staring at the two of us. We tried to sit close to the group of children, but everyone withdrew from us.

All the kids went right to sleep afterward. Maybe marijuana was used in the soup. After we ate we went back and slept on the ground. My friend had a scarf that was torn. I used my own torn scarf to cover my head so the rice seed couldn't get in my ears. My friend told me she wanted to escape. I told her I wanted to escape also or to sneak out to see my parents. She told me if something happened to her to take her stuff to her parents. She had family pictures, jewelry, and American dollars buried in a hole, and she showed it to me that night.

I also had a hole, but there was nothing left in it. "If something happens, take care of my belongings for me," she whispered. She was crying. I told her, "Don't say that. If something happens to you it will happen to me because we are friends." Her face was very pale and her hands were shaking. We swore to each other that we would take care of each other's families. She took her torn, dirty scarf and tied her wrist to mine. "Don't forget," she cried. I couldn't keep my eyes open and fell asleep.

It was very dark, rainy, and cold. I heard a noise. I didn't know if I was dreaming or if it really happened. All I know is that my friend, who had tied herself to me, was gone. I tried to ask some of the children if they knew where she was. I asked the soldiers, "Did you see the comrade who slept next to me?" One of the soldiers told me, "Get your ass out of here and go to sleep like death." I went back and lay down. I was shaking.

The soldiers were so angry, I was afraid that I would be next. Three men came and stood at my feet. They threw a pair of dirty green pants covered with blood in my face. Then they threw a bra and a black shirt covered in her blood. "Here. If you have compassion and empathy for her, you can go with her." They were drunk. They had raped her. They were like animals. They accused me of not sharing with Angka. I begged them, saying I only work hard for Angka. I bowed to them. They told each other, "Let her eat and get strong and then we will do the same thing to her as what we did to her friend." They turned to me and said, "We will send you to eat dirt." My friend was gone. They forced me to wear her clothes. I was transferred again to another place.

Sometimes laughing is better than crying. Every day was a horrible day for us. We were always worrying, starving, and so afraid that we would die. I prayed for it not to get dark. This happened every day from 1975 until 1979. Today I still have nightmares. I feel sad when the sun sets.

I feel that I am blessed and very fortunate. I work in a place that helps refugees and have met people who understand what I have been through. I believe we must tell people what happened to us during the Pol Pot years–the killing, starvation, and torture. I feel sad and very sorrowful for my sister and brother-in-law, my friends, and fellow Cambodians who didn't make it through those cruel and inhumane times. Even today, because of what happened to me, I sometimes feel as if I am again living in the darkness. Still, sometimes when it rains, or when darkness falls, my mind is their prisoner and I struggle to be free.

This is dedicated to the memory of my sister and brother-in-law, Sy Lay and Thou Kim Noev. It is also in memory of my cousin Hing Tith and his family, and the rest of my family and friends who were murdered by the Khmer Rouge.

SARAH P. TUN (at right, with her family) moved to Houston after her father applied for sponsorship from the International Rescue Committee there. The family lived in Texas for about two years then moved to Modesto, California, where they have been living since 1982. She goes to school full time and works part time. In spring 1996 she graduated from California State University at Stanislaus with a bachelor's degree in sociology. She plans to get a master's degree in social work.

❀ ❀ ❀

# A Four-Year-Old's View
# of the Khmer Rouge

### SARAH P. TUN

Mom, are we almost at Grandma's house? I'm really hungry and tired," I asked my mom on April 17, 1975, when the Khmer Rouge took over Phnom Penh. The twelve- to fourteen–year–old Khmer Rouge soldiers, wearing black outfits and black shoes made of car tires, forced all the people in the city to walk in two straight lines. When we left the city, we didn't have many things with us. We had no food supplies or clothes. I remember walking barefoot on the hot sidewalk. My feet were blistering. Sweat was dripping down my face. I kept asking my parents, "Why do we have to walk for so long without resting and with no food to eat?"

All of a sudden I heard gunshots. Babies cried and people screamed. I saw blood dripping from one man's head. I grabbed my aunt's arm and screamed. She told me to be quiet and that everything would be all right. As we walked farther I saw bodies lying on the sidewalk. One of the soldiers said, "If you want to live, do as you are told and don't stop walking." People ran for their lives. The wounded ones were killed by the Khmer Rouge soldiers or were left on the sidewalk to die.

At dusk we reached a town. The villagers were very nice. They gave us food and a place to stay for the night. We slept until dawn, when the Khmer Rouge soldiers came and forced us to move along. We walked during the day, and at night we would sleep in the fields. We had walked about two weeks when we reached another town. By this time, about half the people were gone. Some had died of starvation and illness. Some had been killed and some had been forced to other villages. The people who were living in the cities were called the April 17th people. The April 17th people lived under harsh rules. The villagers watched us like hawks. We were treated like criminals.

Under Khmer Rouge rule, all private property was outlawed. Cooking at home was outlawed. Everything from work to sex to family life was tightly controlled. Everyone in the villages was supposed to eat together in a central mess hall called the common kitchen. They gave us only milky-white water porridge twice a day.

At this time, my family was separated. My father was imprisoned because he was suspected of being in the military during the Lon Nol reign. My mother and baby brother were sent to another camp. My oldest brother was sent to a camp for children who were about his age. My sister and I were put into an orphan's home. I was four years old and my sister was three. We each had only one skirt and one blouse. We lived on the second floor. We were afraid of ghosts because there were so many dead people around the village. We were so skinny. We never had enough to eat. Sometimes we ate raw grain.

My sister and I used to run to our mother's camp, which was about thirty miles from the orphan's home. Sometimes we got caught and punished. We were lucky because they didn't kill us. They warned my mother that if we did this again they would kill the whole family. We stayed at the orphan's home for about two years without seeing our family.

One day the Khmer Rouge soldiers gathered all the April 17th people into trucks. They didn't tell us where we were going. Some of the old people were crying because they knew that we were going to die. The second camp they brought us to was worse than the first camp. The Khmer Rouge soldiers were very mean. Sometimes they gave us nothing to eat. By this time many people had started stealing food from Angka. Sometimes I would go to the rice field and try to catch fish.

I remember one time my oldest brother caught some catfish from the rice field and the soldiers were chasing after him. He ran home and hid under the banana leaves. The soldiers asked my mother if she had seen a boy with a bunch of fish running through there. My mother replied, "I did not see any boy run through here." "If you lie to us we will kill you all!" the soldiers threatened her. They began searching the house, but they didn't find my brother.

A lot of children were dying from starvation and disease because there was no medicine available. I was one of the children who was going to die. I had pneumonia and had no one to care for me. My mother's only choice was to take me to the hospital and leave me there. At the hospital there was very little medicine. Some was in Pepsi bottles filled with dark liquid. One of the nurses came over and gave me a shot. She told my mother to leave me there and go back to work because there was nothing she could do to help me. As she left me I could see tears rolling down her cheeks.

They put me on a mat next to another girl. They told me to go to sleep. The next day my health was worse than ever. They gave me some pills to take. The pills were about the size of my thumb. The pills didn't help me. Two days later my mother came to see me. She had already worked for a few hours. When I saw her, I started to cry. She shaved my hair off, gave me a bath, and gave me some aspirin that had been given to her by a friend who used to be a nurse. My health soon improved.

In late December 1978 the Vietnamese invaded Cambodia. By this time, my family was together again. I was in the rice fields trying to catch fish when I heard gunshots and bombs exploding from very far away. The noise came closer and closer to our camp. I saw stampeding cows. People were screaming and running for shelter. I ran home and asked my parents what was going on. They didn't know. My father gathered our family together and ran down to the creek. It had no water, but we stayed in the creek bed for a couple of hours with other families. When the shooting slowed down, the men went out to gather food from the kitchen. It was the first time that we had had a decent meal since the Khmer Rouge took over.

A few weeks later we gradually moved back to Phnom Penh. On our way we saw a lot of dead people lying in the ditches and rice fields. Before we reached Phnom Penh we saw a man lying dead on the sidewalk. He was wearing a black outfit, tire shoes, and dark glasses. His motorcycle lay next to him. His left leg was bent, and blood oozed out of his thigh and head. As people walked past him they spit and threw rocks. He was a Khmer Rouge soldier. I had nightmares about this man. Sometimes I still have nightmares about this ghost.

My little brother was born while we were returning from Phnom Penh. There were no doctors or nurses, and there was no medicine to take. When we reached Phnom Penh we felt much safer than we had in the rural areas because the Vietnamese soldiers protected us from the Khmer Rouge.

On November 15, 1979, a friend of my father's told us about the refugee camps in Thailand. He said, "You should go there because the United Nations High Commission for Refugees [UNHCR] provides medicine, food, and clothing for your family." When my father heard this good news he quickly arranged transportation to visit the camps to see if it was true. He planned to go by himself at first. He prepared an old ten–speed bicycle for the trip, but on the night he was to leave Phnom Penh there was a big storm. It rained for three days and three nights, and the streets were flooded. One week later his friend told him that a truck was supposed to be available for my family to escape to the Thai camps.

We rode in a truck that was full of rice bags. After we got off the truck we stayed in the dense forest during the day and we walked at night. My father had to hire a guide to lead us through the rain forest in the mountains.

By one o'clock in the morning, everyone who was going with the guide assembled in a long line stretching from his house. It was a starry night. A crescent moon hung in the western sky, and it was very quiet, except for the crickets. We began to walk much more slowly than we would have liked on the footpath, then on an oxcart path, through rice fields and then jungle.

Along the way to the camps there were many dangerous situations. My father told us to walk exactly in his footsteps. We walked cautiously around a bend and came upon the site of an explosion. It was a blood–spattered scene, with an arm hanging from a tree branch, part of a leg caught in the bamboo. Ten or more dead people lay by the side of the path. Many more were wounded. Mines went off everywhere. It was a terrible way to die or be maimed after living through the Khmer Rouge years and coming so close to freedom. Besides the mines, there were robberies, rapes, and murders along the way. My family and I walked through the forest for about twenty–four hours, until we reached the Thai border. We arrived at the Thai camps with horrible memories of the Khmer Rouge.

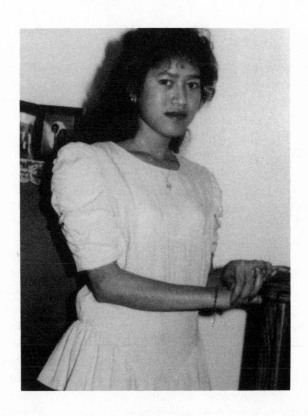

NAVY DY and her family escaped from Battambang at the end of 1979 and reached Khao-I-Dang refugee camp. After two years at the camp Navy and her family were sponsored by her uncle with the help of a church organization. They went to another camp in the Philippines for seven months before landing in San Diego. After three months in California, Navy was placed in ninth grade. After high school she attended community college for two years. She then married and moved to Virginia. She found a full-time job at a congressional office in Washington, D.C., and she now works at the Pentagon.

---

# The Tragedy of My Homeland

NAVY DY

I was born in 1966 in the city of Battambang. There are seven children in my family–two younger and older sisters, and two older brothers. We are all in the U.S.A., but my father isn't.

When the country fell we were forced to move to the countryside called Moung, on the western side of Battambang. Because there was no auto transportation, we had to travel by foot and drag everything we could. On our painful trip we saw many swelling corpses; some had been dead a long time and others had died recently. Most died from traveling, and others were killed by Khmer Rouge comrades. Not only were we scared of these comrades, but were emotionally sick from these tragic scenes.

After five days of this struggling trip we got to Moung with only a bag full of clothes. When I got to that village I saw only a few small houses, rice fields, and small irrigation ditches. We had to build our own camp under a mango tree with the other ten families by using every scrap of our old clothes and plastic. Later, my father built a small barn for us. Moung was supposed to be a very poor land. There was no river water, but a small pit with very dirty water; no orchids or fruit trees or even soil, but an empty desert with a few mango trees.

About 300 families moved to this place, but three-quarters of them died from disease, starvation, and harsh, bloody torture. Because many of the people in the camp were official workers for the government, we were treated like the Khmer Rouge's enemies. My father was one of them.

After two months at Moung things were getting worse and worse. All of my family were treated like prisoners. My older sisters and my older brothers were assigned to the mountain of Phnom Tippedey. My father was assigned somewhere, but he never returned. I was told he was killed by the ruthless Khmer Rouge soldiers.

Only three of us stayed with my mom. My two younger sisters were five and six, and I was eight years old. We all worked like adults for only a bowlful of rice soup. As I remember it, my mom told me there were many killings around our area, at the rice fields and farms close by where she worked. At night she saw a group of Chinese trucks come to pick up a whole bunch of sacks of rice. The Communist comrades told us, "We don't have enough food now because other villagers are in need." We already knew this was nonsense, but we had to keep quiet, otherwise I could have become one of the skeletons that my mom saw every day in the rice fields.

Two years later, after all the struggle and many hardships, we were again forced to be separated from my mom because we were put into another girls group. I turned eleven, and my other two sisters were now seven and eight. We were assigned to stay in a youth group called Kong Koma. Because we were so young and never had stayed away from our mom, we were terrified.

The camp we stayed at was about a quarter-mile away from my mom's camp and in the woods. Fortunately, we stayed together, but we had to build our own tent, which was made from scraps of small branches from trees and some old clothes from my mom. When the wind or rain came, we were wet and cold.

Sometimes we sneaked out to stay with my mom and left

at five o'clock in the morning to get back to the youth camp. If we didn't, the punishment would be harsh. We would get a few slaps or no food for a day. We might even be tied up against a tree waiting to be tortured. If worse came to worse, our parents could be suffocated with a plastic bag wrapped around their heads. Because the places were so dirty we had to shave our heads to eliminate lice. Most people got sick. People died every day.

After a five-month stay at this place my sisters and I were so sick that we were permitted to go back to my mom. Part of my sister's body swelled and other parts were so bony. Her hair was hardly growing. When she went to the bathroom her stool was mostly blood. I knew she wouldn't live much longer. My mom got old-fashioned medicine, which was made from scrapings of the roots of wild trees. Usually it tasted terrible and made her throw up. My mom had to try everything for her. Fortunately, weeks later she got better and better.

During the Vietnamese invasion at the beginning of 1979, my family, except for my father, was reunited. After all of my experiences, I can only say that our lives are full of miracles. Only one question stays in my mind: Why did Khmer people kill other Khmers in our own motherland, Cambodia? I hope that these experiences will teach us some lessons and show the world how much we have been suffering so that our children will remember.

I dedicate this to all the spirits of innocent Cambodian people, especially to my father, who died without his family, without our respect or our mercy.

*RATHA DUONG (a pen name) was sponsored by the Hebrew Immigrant Aid Society in New York and then moved to St. Paul, Minnesota, in 1981. She is married and has two children and is getting a master's degree in social work. Ratha is a social worker for the Wilder Foundation Social Adjustment Program for Southeast Asia.*

# Hurt, Pain, and Suffering

## RATHA DUONG

On April 18, 1975, the Khmer Rouge took over Pursat province. On April 20, 1975, at ten o'clock, the sound of guns was heard everywhere in the city. The Communist soldiers walked all over the place. They told us to leave the city. My parents rented a cart to carry our belongings to the countryside. More guns were heard. People ran and ran. Children cried for their parents. The cries of people and animals mixed together.

Angka started to take action. They put people in groups of twenty families. Each member of the group had a job to do. My father belonged to a men's group that plowed the rice fields. My sister and I joined the mobile girls group. My brother joined the mobile boys group. The rest of my sisters and brothers stayed at the orphanage children's center. Only my mother, my baby sister, and my baby brother stayed home.

My mother lost weight because of depression, stress, not enough sleep, and lack of food. One evening when I came back from work I saw my father carrying my baby brother while he was cooking. It was unusual to see my father cook and my mother asleep on the bamboo bed with the blanket covering her body. Then I heard my mother calling my father, "Honey! Where are our children? Please bring them in." All my sisters and brothers cried and gathered around her quickly. The baby cried because he needed breast milk. She took the baby and fed him. She cried with sorrow and said to my father, "Honey, we have been married almost twenty years. We have a good marriage and we have good children. When I die, please take care of our children. They are our treasures."

"Mom, please don't say this. You must live with us, take care of us. We need you, Mom!" I cried. My father looked stunned when he heard my mother say this, but he turned to my brother and said, "Nal, run quick to fetch Grandmother!" All the children cried out and embraced our mother until Grandmother came. Grandmom was shocked when she saw my mother, and she asked her, "What happened?" She then called my father to find a monk.

Outside, the sky was full of black clouds, and there were no stars. Thunder followed the piercing lightning. It started to sprinkle a little. An owl perched on the roof and cried. My grandmother cried and shared many memories with my mother. I was the only one who stayed awake with my mother. All my brothers and sisters fell asleep next to her with faces full of tears. At nine in the evening my mother's face looked so awful. Suddenly she sat up and asked for water. I gave her water, and her body started twisting. She asked for my baby brother. My grandmother let her hold the baby. She fed the baby. Her legs became cold.

My father and the monk came. The monk shook his head and prayed for her. By the time he finished praying, I no longer heard my mother's voice. The monk took the baby away from Mother's breast. At ten o'clock on June 15, 1975, the monk pronounced her dead. She was thirty-seven.

My grandmother and I cried out and woke up all my sisters and brothers. The hut was full of horrible voices of the children.

It was very difficult for me, my father, and all the children to face reality. All my brothers and sisters asked me what happened to Mother. I had no answer besides tears on my face. My mother was gone forever and would never return to us. I had no milk for the baby. I made rice soup for him, and my father, after working many hours, traveled from one place to another to ask for sugar to put into the rice soup for him. The baby cried day and night for milk. He lost a lot of weight. One night, at midnight, I heard the baby making snoring sounds. Many bubbles of blood came out through his nose. In August 1975, at five months old, my brother died.

In October 1976 there was starvation all over the place. I saw dead bodies everywhere. The smell was awful because nobody buried the bodies. I was so skinny. I could count all the bones in my body and my eyes were sunken deep into my face. Besides the starvation, Angka tortured and executed teachers, students, soldiers, and ex–government people. New jails opened everywhere. Angka placed travel restrictions and guarded each community.

While I was planting rice I saw three soldiers walking toward the men's group, which was plowing the rice field. The soldier called a man from the field. I was in shock. The man was my uncle. The soldier tied my uncle's hands behind his back and forced him to walk. His face looked pale and panicked. The soldiers beat him on the side of his head with a gun, and blood came out of his nose and mouth as they pushed him away.

The next morning I heard that the soldiers had arrested his wife and their baby to reeducate them. Late in the evening I decided to stop at my great–aunt's home to let her know what had happened to my uncle. A short distance in front of me I heard steps. I hid myself in the bushes near the street. I was about twenty yards from her house.

I could see inside through the palm leaf wall of her hut. She lay on the bamboo floor and breastfed her baby. Her husband and five small children sat in a circle, drinking something under the light of a fish-oil lamp. Two soldiers with guns went to the front door and three soldiers were at the back door. It was happening again. I saw the soldiers tie my great-uncle. All the children were scared and screaming out. I began to sweat. I held my breath and closed my eyes. They tied up the entire family, one by one, and kicked them out of the hut. Then they pushed them into a cart and drove away.

In November and early December 1976 there was no food to eat. I was sick. I asked myself when I was going to die. Would I die by starvation or by torture? I thought that if I died, I would no longer have to work like an animal. I asked my group leader for permission to rest one day. She said no. So I worked in the field planting rice. My legs were weak from standing in the mud. The rain fell hard and my body shook with chills. My eyes couldn't see. I felt dizzy, and then I collapsed into the mud. I heard the group leader tell girls to carry me out under the tree. I was unconscious.

When I woke up my body felt hot, and I didn't see anyone around me. Instead of going back with the mobile girls I went to see my father, who stayed with his mobile team. I walked like a turtle across the rice field. I sat down every hundred yards on a dike. Out of nowhere I heard a young child cry for help. I stood up a little bit and saw a boy about seven being hit by a Communist soldier. I sat back down and crawled inside the rice paddy to hide from the soldier. He walked past me, and then I saw the wounds and blood all over the boy's body. I thought it was my brother at first.

I continued to walk when the soldier was gone. I caught

some crabs along the way for my father. Two bulls were close by, eating rice. I pulled them away from the rice because if Angka caught them eating they would kill the person who was supposed to be taking care of them. I then heard a sound next to the bulls. I walked toward the mysterious sound and found my father. He had fallen down in the mud and couldn't get up. I pulled his arm and legs from the mud, but I was so weak that I fell down over him. Luckily, I still had the bull line in my hand. When the bull pulled on the line, we were able to get up from the mud. I took my krama and cleaned my father with water. We walked toward his hut with the two bulls. I fixed crab soup for him to eat.

I stayed overnight with my father. He told me that he had met one of his former students, who worked as a rice keeper next to my community, about ten miles away. Then he fell asleep because he was exhausted. I thought of all the times my father had taken care of me when I was sick. Now it was my opportunity to get him rice from his old student. At five in the morning, while my father still slept, I woke up and decided to go to get some rice. I walked across the rice field because I didn't have a permission letter to travel.

At sunset, I finally reached the community my father spoke of. I saw a light at the main kitchen. As I walked to the kitchen I stepped on a dead palm leaf. The sound was heard by the lady who was serving rice to Khmer Rouge soldiers. Two men ran toward me. They arrested me and brought me to the lady, who accused me of being a thief. The two men tied my arms behind my back and took me to the soldier's station. It was dark. There was no moon in the sky. I felt sad for myself that this happened.

The soldiers put me in a jail that looked like a cage. I heard a girl next to my cage cry with sorrow, and I smelled the stench of blood. In the morning I didn't see the prison-

❀

97

ers, except for the girl. I told her not to cry. We heard the mean voice of a lady. In her hand she held a bowl of rice soup for my friend. Instead of giving it to her to eat, that witch poured the rice soup on the girl's hair. The rice soup dripped through her hair, and she tried to reach it with her tongue while the witch laughed. Then I saw the girl's body shake, her mouth open and her eyes staring at me. She died calling my name. I cried without tears. Two soldiers came to remove her body. Only later did I realize that this was one of my high school friends. She was the only good friend I had.

One hour later a soldier took me to another room far from my cage. That room was a little dark and full of plastic bags. The stench of blood on the walls filled the room. I didn't think I'd have a chance to see my father, who was waiting for my rice. Two men came with a gun. I closed my eyes. I knew they were going to hurt me. When I opened my eyes I recognized one of the soldiers. He was my father's ex-student. He saw me and said to his colleague that I was innocent. Then he gave me a couple cans of rice for my father.

In the afternoon I arrived at my father's hut. I saw only my sister, who was crying in front of the hut. I asked her where Father was. She told me that he had died. I was afraid and trembling. He did not wait for me to get the rice. I dug the ground to bury him. I took my scarf and his scarf and wrapped them around his body. My sister and brother carried his head and I carried his legs. We buried him. We bowed our heads and saluted him good-bye. In December 1976 my father died at the age of forty-three. He left behind eight children. My sister, brother, and I wailed with hopelessness.

After the death of my father I became an angry person. I hated living in the Khmer Rouge community. Every place I went, I always dreamed about my parents, my family, and the happiness we all had shared. I was mad at Angka, who broke my family apart. I always volunteered to work far away from the community. I longed for the day that I would be away from Angka, away from the Khmer Rouge, away from the sadness.

*KHUON KIV escaped from Cambodia in 1979 with a few older friends. They arrived at the Surin Camp, which was under U.N. control. He stayed there for three months with orphaned children. When the Thai government tried to deport the children back to Cambodia, the U.N. did as much as possible to find a sponsor for them. Khuon landed in Georgia in 1979 after being sponsored by a Laotian organization. Later he was sponsored by relatives of the family that came with him from Thailand. They lived in Virginia. Khuon then attended community college. Four years later he was offered a full-time job at Congress in Washington, D.C., as a machine operator. He worked for eleven years, until his department was abolished when the Republicans took over the House of Representatives. He is receiving technical training in the hopes of becoming a computer technician. Khuon lives in Riverdale, Maryland. He is married and has one son.*

*❀  ❀  ❀*

# The Darkness of My Experience

### KHUON KIV

I was born in 1961 in the Battambang province. There were five in our family. My father passed away in 1972. One of my older sisters disappeared at the beginning of the war in 1969, but she was found later, in 1985. When the Communists took over Battambang on April 18, 1975, there were only three members left in my family: my mom, my older sister, and me.

After thousands of people were evacuated from the city, my family lived in a village about one mile away. Soon afterward, my sister and I were assigned to the labor camp in a youth group called Kong Chalat. My mom was at a different village. She had to stay by herself. At that time my sister was nineteen and I was thirteen years old.

After the separation I was terrified, lonely, and living mostly with strangers at strange places. This Kong Chalat group was supposed to work harder, be emotionally persistent, and to be a role model for all ages. We basically dug irrigation ditches and planted rice. At my age, we should have been attending school and living in a decent home with food to eat. But instead we were forced to work ten to twelve hours a day with only a bowlful of rice soup and had to sleep on the ground.

The camps usually were made from scraps of small branches of trees. My mosquito net and blanket were made from old clothes. When it rained I usually got wet and was pretty cold. At night the camp was somewhat quiet, and you could hear many scary sounds, such as foxes howling and rattlesnakes hissing.

We always were assigned to guard our camp because the Communist government soldiers, whom we called Angka, made us not trust each other. We had to watch one another. One night it was my turn to guard the camp. It was about 8:30 P.M., but I could see some shadows. As I heard a digging sound about an eighth of a mile away from my camp, I sneaked out and looked. I saw about ten to fifteen people digging dirt. Some were tied up, blindfolded, with their mouths covered, while others carried chopping shovels on their shoulders.

Suddenly, I heard a voice screaming in pain. "Oy! Oy!" echoed through the woods. It was the sound of a human screaming for help because he just had been hit with a shovel by young Khmer Rouge soldiers who could have been the victim's sons or relatives. It was the sound of living hell, the sound of a really frightening nightmare that we usually only hear in a movie.

A moment later the sound was getting softer and softer, and that was the end of it. I was so scared and shaky that I went to get my friend up. Not only was he not surprised, but his response made me more nervous. He told me, "You better be quiet or we will be next."

The bloody voice of the victim terrified me, but my friend's phrase was even more scary. These voices will haunt me forever. For months I could hear them every time I fell asleep.

During my stay I noticed that many more people were missing every day. They either got sick and died or went to see Angka and never returned. The Khmer Rouge slang was, "You will be the soil for the rice field."

One year later it was my turn to get assigned to a place that made me nervous. I was sure that it was the end of my life. I couldn't sleep, talk, or even eat, although I was always hungry. When the morning came, the faces of all my campmates looked so pale and scared, including mine. As time passed by, fortunately we were assigned to somewhere in the jungle near Angkor Wat where we were supposed to collect wood and rubber from the rubber trees.

The jungle was supposed to be the most unsafe and dangerous place in the country. There were poisonous insects, tigers, elephants, and dangerous snakes. About two hundred people were assigned there from different villages, but many had been killed or had gotten very sick. One month later I was very sick with malaria. Because there was no medicine, hospitals, or even nurses around, I had to do everything I could to survive. I even drank old wild tree leaves by grinding them. I rubbed myself with a coin and hoped that I would get better, but I never did.

Weeks later my illness was getting worse and worse. Not only did I feel pain from the disease, but I was scared of a thousand different things. I also missed my family. Finally Angka transferred me to a hospital with ten other people. The hospital was an old building with only some old-fashioned medicine, a few slightly trained nurses, and beds. When I got there I wondered if I would survive again. In fact, I thought I actually died once. As I remember, part of my body swelled and other parts were so bony. I couldn't move, eat, or sleep for weeks.

I was given an IV with the medicine in a Pepsi bottle instead of in an airtight plastic bag. The IV was made from coconut water. Not only was the hospital too crowded, but many patients were bony and swollen, like corpses. They lay around me on the floor for weeks. Every day many patients died and more poured into the hospital from different places.

Three months later, even though there was no nutrition, beds, medicine, nurses, or doctors, some were still alive, including myself. Amazingly, human life still beat the odds.

After all of these nightmares of bloodletting, skeletons in the rice fields, and swelling corpses floating everywhere in the Tonle Sap River, which I witnessed at my early age, the memory of this event still haunts me. I would like to dedicate this to the spirits of all innocent Khmer people, especially to my sister and my mom, who died during this time. I also dedicate it to my young son, Anthony Veasna Kiv, so that the Cambodian people's suffering and struggle will not be forgotten.

GEN L. LEE *came in April 1980 with her family to the United States from a Red Cross refugee camp in Thailand. They were sponsored by several families from a Catholic church in Birmingham, Michigan. She now lives in Laguna Hills, California, and is completing her thesis for a master of arts degree in Asian American studies at the University of California at Los Angeles. She also is writing a book about her family's ordeal in Cambodia and in the Thai refugee camps, and about their initial experiences in the United States. She plans to pursue a Ph.D. in history, concentrating on Southeast Asia, specifically modern Cambodian history. She hopes to become a scholar and to teach at a university.*

❀  ❀  ❀

# *Survival in Spite of Fear*

## GEN L. LEE

One morning in mid–April 1975, Father was driving his moped to Mother's birthplace, about a half–hour ride from Battambang city. Sitting between my parents, I realized that many people were frantically moving in every direction, but I did not know what was going on. No one ever had told me that fighting existed before this day. At seven, I was too young to comprehend the complexities of society. War and hunger never entered my mind because my life was sheltered and I was well provided for. Suddenly, when the Khmer Rouge took over, Cambodia was plunged into an abyss of darkness that was infested with hunger, disease, work exhaustion, and evildoers.

I was sent to the female youth working unit, which marked the beginning of separation and isolation from my family and the beginning of hell. After being separated from my family, my first duty as daughter of Angka was to carry water up the slope from the river in Battambang in order to water peppers and other vegetables.

My unit transplanted and replanted rice and harvested the grains. There were times as I would smack a handful of rice plants against the side of my foot that I would fall forward into the thick brown water. My body was light, and I was unable to balance myself against the heavy mud that came with the roots from the rice. We were forced to build

dams and trenches. Every day we overworked our malnour-
ished bodies. My unit was always on the move, working on different projects that were usually never completed. I stood in
water most of the time, which contributed to my early arthritis.

I dreaded the bell that would ring at dawn, knowing that
revolutionary propaganda songs would follow. As a child I
had no sense of time and space. All I knew for over three
years was that hunger and death were forever present. All I
cared about was food, and sometimes I did not want to live.

Rations of food were meager. Except for the few occasions when rice was provided, the usual ration was no more
than a bowl of water with a few grains of rice. But this was
better than nothing. It tasted like fine cuisine. It was difficult to work more than ten hours a day on an empty stomach. I ate creatures and wild fruits and vegetables that I
would not have eaten during better times. I was not good at
catching field rats and frogs. Snails, crabs, and tiny fish were
easier to catch and hide.

When the rice fields were plowed, snails would float to
the top and crabs would be uprooted from their safe places.
Every time I stuck my arm in a crab hole I worried that a
snake would bite me. Snakes provided excellent sources of
nutrition and medicine for people who dared to catch them.
Whenever my hands and stomach were empty I looked at
others' food like a predator eyeing its prey.

When it rained my body shivered like a tiny chick yearning for its mother's protection and warmth. My body was
reduced to bones and skin, a thin frame that could easily fall
when caught in the wind. One time everyone in my camp
was given a rare opportunity to return to her village, but
instead of being happy and grateful, I had to be forced by
the youth captain to go. Because of the pouring rain, wind,
darkness (I was afraid of ghosts), and my tiredness, I didn't
think it was worth the effort.

That evening as I walked against the strong wind my
skeleton of a figure slipped and fell countless times into the

mud. Although it was cool only during the wet seasons, the cold wind often chilled through the bones of my damp body. When it rained my unit built a fire to warm our flesh and to dry the clothes on our body. There was no extra set of clothes to change. We worked rain or shine.

Starvation and overwork were only two agents of death. Countless forms of disease conquered the lives of many. Malaria would have taken mine were it not for the mercy of the gods and my mother's undying love and care. Risking her own life, she walked far and traded gold for medicine and made offerings to the gods to save my soul.

Because of fear and naiveté, I nearly died from work exhaustion. Building a dam and trenches was not suited for someone under four feet with a bony figure. I was stupid enough to stand at the front of the line, where the baskets were fuller with dirt. If I had been smarter I would have stood at the end, because by the time the baskets reached me, most of the dirt would have fallen off and I would have been holding less weight. It just so happened that one day Mother was working close by, and during her break she came close enough to see my emaciated frame. Choked with tears and brokenhearted, she returned to her camp and vowed to save me from the grip of death.

107

My mother's team leader was taking orders from Angka, but she was also my mother's friend and a mother herself (her daughter was my group leader). She was sympathetic. I was too small for my age. The leader instructed Mother how to get me out of my work unit, and so we proceeded to execute her plan. It was like a drama. She knew that Angka would send young Khmer Rouge cadres to fetch me if I didn't return to camp after a permitted visit. When they did come, I made a scene, crying and kicking uncontrollably while Mother tried her best to make me go back, pretending that it was me who refused to go. This way Mother would not be at fault, because punishment for adults was more severe than for children.

Fortunately, the plan worked, and I was able to stay with my mother. From then on I followed my mother's unit, along with my younger sister, and only did such light duties as babysitting and gathering vegetables for the mess hall. This was after 1977, the year of the purges of cadres within the Khmer Rouge leadership.

Sometime in 1978, miraculously, Mother was reassigned to planting and raising vegetables, fruits, and other food. We moved into the farm and built a tiny open hut without doors. Mother purposely did this to ward off any suspicion of stealing "community property." Of course, she did "steal" what she planted and shared the food with her parents and siblings. My older brother, who was stuck with his work unit, occasionally received some food from her. For nearly a year our measly rice and porridge rations were supplemented by fruits that Mother would hide in her tiny hut.

During most of those four years both Mother and Father went to the frontier. My older brother was in a unit of his age group. Except for Father, my family was united after the Vietnamese invasion. Dad did not return until weeks after Vietnam pushed the Khmer Rouge into the forest. We moved back to our native village, but poor harvests, the impending famine, and the continued fighting between the Khmer Rouge and Vietnamese forces sent us not only out of town but eventually out of the country. In fact, my family and more than fifty close relatives were caught in the crossfire, sheltering ourselves from bombs and mortar shells, barely escaping the new turmoil.

My mother, who possesses great vision and resourcefulness, did not trust either the Khmer Rouge or the Vietnamese because they were Communists. She felt that Cambodia would not recover its stability and prosperity any time soon. Almost immediately after the invasion my family, along with relatives and thousands of other Cambodians, trekked into the refugee camps in Thailand.

We had to cross the border three times. On the first attempt we were robbed by bandits and abandoned in the forest. My family then walked into a temporary refugee camp on the Thai border. But less than two months later we were forced to return to Cambodia through the Dangrek Mountains, where land mines and corpses awaited approximately 45,000 displaced Cambodians.

After about two months of walking barefoot in the summer heat with little food, we finally reached the place for which we originally had started, an area on the border where we could quickly cross into Thailand again. An honest man safely guided my family to an old refugee camp in Thailand, where we stayed for two days before being sent to another camp.

Today, seventeen years later, I have a great desire to visit the land of my birth and somehow, someday, contribute to rebuilding the country of my early childhood. I have been delaying plans to return because of political instability, banditry, and continued fighting between the government and Khmer Rouge forces. In my studies and private thoughts I often wonder why the Khmer Rouge leaders are not brought to trial in the International Court of Law. How much longer must the Cambodian people endure the pains of today and mourn the loss of yesterday? Aren't two and a half decades of war and hunger enough? Cambodians must stop killing Cambodians and Cambodia for the sake of power, personal gain, and ideology.

109

*SUSIE HEM and her family in 1982 moved to a Thai refugee camp, where they lived for a year. In 1983 she was sponsored by the friend of one of her parents. She arrived in Provo, Utah, on November 3, 1983. She now lives in Long Beach, California. She works as a beautician and has her own shop called Leng's Beauty Salon.*

# *Pol Pot*

### SUSIE HEM

In 1975, I was only five years old. Pol Pot forced all of the people in Phnom Penh to move out of their homes to live in poor farm areas. Pol Pot's soldiers told us that we were going to move out for only three days and that we didn't need to bring all of our property with us. They lied.

During the four years under Pol Pot, most people lived without enough food, water, clothing, or shelter. We had to eat porridge every day. We had to find food on our own time in order to survive, and we ate anything, including banana trees and all kinds of leaves that weren't poison. I ate snails, snakes, grasshoppers, crickets, and crabs.

I remember that one night my mom and I sneaked out to find some food in a small cabin that was used as a kitchen. We found a blob of rice and brought some home. Mom cooked just enough for both of us, and she wrapped the rest in a plastic bag and buried it in the ground. We also buried our jewelry because when we ran out of food, we traded it for rice, meat, and medicine.

Pol Pot forced all of us to work. If someone didn't work hard, he or she would be killed in front of other people. We worked from five in the morning until dark. We got to rest for only ten minutes, twice a day.

We dug dirt and built dams to block out water during the rainy season. Some people worked with fertilizer. The women ground rice and cut it. Pol Pot forced children from five years old to work. Elderly women stayed home and took care of the children who were under five years old.

My mom was separated from my father. Every two months she would sneak out to meet him so they could talk about running away from this place and find another place with more food and water. We always wanted to run away to a safe place, but all places were the same, with beatings, killings, and people dying of hunger.

Every night when I went to sleep I heard gunshots. Every night many families were being killed by Pol Pot's soldiers because they were accused of being Chinese, Vietnamese, or in Lon Nol's former army. Pol Pot killed my mom's friend and her whole family after accusing them of being Chinese.

There was a man who was friends with a woman, and they had a friendly chat under a tree. Pol Pot saw them and accused them of having an affair. Pol Pot took them to be questioned. The man and woman said that they were only friends, but Pol Pot didn't believe them. Pol Pot tied them up on a cross and then told everyone to watch the couple being questioned and hit. The lady was pregnant and was hit until she lost the baby and died. The man also was beaten to death.

In 1979 the Vietnamese came to Cambodia. We were freed from Pol Pot's dictatorship and rudeness. We lived in Sisophon for a year and tried to escape to Thailand, but my father got caught by the Vietnamese and was thrown into jail. My mother bailed him out and they started a small business. We continued to run our business for two years before we tried to escape again. We finally made it to Thailand in 1982. Once we were in Thailand we had a chance to come to the United States.

On February 4, 1994, I went back to Cambodia. When I arrived there, it was so strange to me because I had grown up in the United States. Cambodia was so dirty, unsanitary, and humid. I saw trash being tossed out into the streets. People drove their cars, motorcycles, and bikes all over the place. They didn't care which direction they went. Poor people begged in the streets, in the markets, and along the houses. They didn't have enough electricity or water. I wanted to help them. I want Cambodia to have a better future.

OUK VILLA moved to Angkor Chei, 40 kilometers east of Kampot, after the Khmer Rouge regime was overthrown. He lived there for nearly a year. In early 1980 he started a new life in Kampot, where he received his general education until 1989. During his academic years he experienced many hardships aside from working both at school and at home. He spent time working as a durian plantation worker, snack seller, horse cart driver, salt field porter, and sugar palm producer. Ouk is a university graduate and works as an English teacher for Veterans International and as administrative assistant for the Taipei Economic and Cultural Representative Office in Phnom Penh.

❀　❀　❀

# *A Bitter Life*

OUK VILLA

On April 17, 1975, the Khmer Republic formally surrendered to the Khmer Rouge and the country was renamed Democratic Kampuchea. My family and other Cambodian families were evacuated from our native homes to the far-off countryside and other rural areas that we never even knew existed.

The first day we were in the new village we were warmly welcomed with a greeting ceremony that included a feast. I was nine then. After the welcome we were given an old thatched hut with a rotten roof. My father had to fix it and replace some walls. Later, we were despised and called the "new" people, and our possessions were taken away for collective use. That same year, people were divided into three types, including the new and the old. The old group had lived in Khmer Rouge–controlled areas before the country's "liberation" and were "full rights" people. Then there were the Khmer Rouge cadres.

We had no private property because everything belonged to Angka and all laws and orders were carried out in the name of Angka. Angka established high-level cooperatives throughout the country with communal eating. No one complained about it and no one spoke badly of Angka. We could speak only in a whisper or in private because we were fearful of being overhead. If they heard us, we would disappear for "reeducation." We were extremely scared of reeducation. It was the only word that everybody knew.

In late 1975 my family was separated. My two sisters were sent to the mobile youth group far away from us. They were forced to work day and night, but they weren't fed enough and they dressed in rags. As for me, I was sent to the child group center, which was about a kilometer from my family. I had to carry manure to the rice fields, and I was badly treated because I was accused of being lazy. From that time on I was not under the care of my parents anymore but was under the control of the unit leaders. We lived in a big house and had to sleep in rows of six, lined up head to toe.

All children had to get up early in the morning or they were kicked and pulled by the unit leaders. We never received any education because schools, money, markets, books, postal services, and religions were banned. The living conditions of the new people grew more desperate and seemed more physically and mentally arduous than the conditions of slaves in the Middle Ages.

We were taught only about hard work and faithfulness to the government. Later we were also taught to call our parents "comrades" and to spy on them.

One night I woke up and looked around to see if everyone was asleep. I walked on tiptoe and climbed down from the house. I ran through the rice fields and the bushes. A couple of times I fell down, and I got many scratches all over my body. Suddenly I saw three men who were tied up and being led by a militiaman to another small bush. From a distance I saw the militiaman force the men to kneel down on the edge of a big pit. A minute later the men were clubbed to death with a hoe. I could see this clearly in the moonlit night. I was terribly frightened and waited for the militiaman to go away.

I scurried to where my parents were. They were fearful of me being noticed and followed by the unit leaders. The next morning, while I was sitting near the window in front of the house, three unit leaders, dressed in black with silk neckerchiefs, approached our hut and said, "Let us bring comrade Villa back to the center." "He is ready to go," said my father. I was shivering with fear, hiding in the house. My father asked me to come out. "Let him follow us," said the big one with a rough voice. Luckily, I was not tied, but I was badly treated and warned. I was very lucky, because any children who escaped or avoided going to the center were tied up and beaten.

Early in 1976 a serious situation arose. My father was separated from my mother and sent to an all-male worksite. My mother was sent to another collective farm to dig canals. As for me, I had to look after cattle on the side of the mountain. My group had to sleep near the cattle. There were strange animal sounds at night, and the wind blowing through the trees scared me.

One night an odd noise woke me up. I was very frightened. What was it? It was a long voice that I had never heard before. It came nearer and nearer. Oh, God! It was under the hut. I screamed and called to my father for help. Everybody jumped up and asked me what was going on. I told them what I had heard. The strange noise came again. I asked them to listen to it. They told me that it was the howl of a wolf, but I didn't know what a wolf was, so I sat shivering with fear and fully awake. Several days later I began to be accustomed to the noises and could sleep well.

❀
117

While I was looking for crickets and grasshoppers to roast one morning, I saw three militiamen lead six people to the edge of an excavation site. The victims were clubbed on their napes with a hoe and they fell into the grave. They weren't dead yet. They were just unconscious in a pool of blood. The militiamen covered the mass grave with soil and some grass. If they had seen me, I would have been killed as well.

In 1977 my mother, my sister, and I were sent to the village again, but not my father. My mother tried to ask other people about him. They told us the devastating news that he had been sent to be reeducated and was not expected to return home. My mother cried and mourned because it meant that he was killed. He was accused of being involved in an anti–Khmer Rouge group, and the head of the village also had found out that he had been a professor in the Lon Nol regime.

There was no doubt that all the people were enemies of and obstacles to the Khmer Rouge government. After my father's death we were spied on all the time and if they had seen or heard any of us complain, we would have been arrested and killed. At night we couldn't talk or walk outside. We had to live in silence.

Early in 1978 my family was separated again. My mother was sent to the widows group, and my sisters were sent to a malarial region where thousands of children died from malaria or from famine and malnutrition. The children had to rely mostly on ineffective traditional herbal remedies.

One day my sisters came from the mobile group. Their faces were haggard, their eyes looked hollow, and their skin was blue. My sisters told our mother how difficult things had been. She hugged them and said nothing, but she shed her tears. I didn't know much about the bitterness of life, but I felt very sad. My two sisters could stay with us only one night. They were starving. We didn't have any food at home. Everything belonged to Angka.

I decided to do something that I didn't want to do. In the morning, before dawn, I got up around four o'clock and went to the collective kitchen to get some tapioca. It was quiet and the cooks were sound asleep. Near the corner of the kitchen there were three big pans full of tapioca, which was used for mixing the gruel. Without waiting, I hurriedly picked up some and packed it in both ends of my blanket and silently went home.

When I got there my mother was so fearful of me being caught. "You would have been killed if you had been arrested, my son. Don't do so again." "Yes, Mom. Never again." I had become a thief because of my sisters' starvation.

In mid-1978 we heard gunfire from the east. Many people escaped from the gunshots. We were excited. After late 1978 children were allowed to return home. My two sisters came back and we lived together, but we were still sad because we missed our father.

A few days later we were ready to pack our belongings and escape from the gunfire. We were evacuated from the village to a mountain called Phnom Thom, which means Big Mountain. We had to walk day and night. I carried my youngest brother on my back. My sisters carried two packs of torn clothing on their heads. My mother carried a bucket of rice on her head. The rice was given to her in the confusion of the war. We stopped only for a short time to rest for meals. At night we slept in the open field. When we set off again, mostly during the night, we walked hand in hand, and sometimes my mother tied a rope to my waist and then to my sisters' waists and she led us together so we wouldn't get lost. I fell down a lot because I kept walking and falling asleep. The string pulled my sisters down, too.

At last we arrived at the side of the mountain. Early one evening, while we were having dinner, we heard gunshots. All around us shells were falling on the ground and exploding. It sounded like hell. A few moments later, we were bombed and fired at. We screamed and my mother prayed to God for help. Why were we being bombed? Why were they shelling us? Have they come to liberate us or kill us? A few seconds later we learned that we were on the front line of the battlefield.

The gunshots finally calmed down, but a lot of people were killed. The ground was covered with blood from the bodies that lay there. Some were dead and some were still alive. Victims lay motionless in pain and agony. Many people mourned over their relatives. Some had been crying and screaming because they couldn't find their children. Fortunately, no one in my family had been killed.

My family and others hurried to get out of there. We arrived at another mountain called Give It Up Mountain. It was very steep and tall. If we could climb over it we could reach Thailand, but we couldn't carry heavy things or children. Some people were forced to climb without their children or belongings. Lots of people fell down and died because they didn't have enough strength to climb. They didn't return to their villages because they were afraid of the Vietnamese soldiers. We had been taught that the Vietnamese would slit our throats if they caught us. But my family and many others decided not to climb the mountain. "I can't live without my children," said my mother. "We must go back to our village. If we die, we'll die together." So we decided to return to the village.

We met thousands of Vietnamese soldiers on our way home. We were very frightened and shocked to see them. They couldn't speak Khmer, but they were very kind and friendly. They gave us rice, sugar, and yellow noodles and let us go to the village safely.

The village was quiet and our hut was burned down, so we built another one the size of a chicken house. It is very hard for a woman with six children to start a new life with her bare hands. We worked hard in the field and had to help our mother plant potatoes and rice.

On January 7, 1979, the Khmer Rouge government in Phnom Penh was dismantled. The Khmer Rouge left thousands widowed, orphaned, and disabled. Sorrow and a profound hatred of the criminal genocidal regime and man's inhumanity to man are deep in our hearts. The sound of the victims' cries of pain and agony are still in our minds. They are asking for justice and are demanding condemnation of the Khmer Rouge butchers.

The Khmer Rouge never stopped committing their atrocities and criminal actions. They are still fighting, killing, and
destroying roads and bridges. This shows that the Khmer
Rouge want another genocide to happen in Cambodia. Never
again must we let the Khmer Rouge return to power!

HONG A. CHORK *came to Washington, D.C., in 1984 from one of the Thai Red Cross refugee camps. He was sponsored by the U.S. Lutheran Social Services in 1984 and classified as an unaccompanied minor. Now a U.S. citizen, Hong lives in Arlington, Virginia. Because of a spinal injury that was undetected until 1989, Hong is handicapped. He is undergoing physical therapy. Hong has successfully trained as a data entry operator and is seeking employment in the Washington, D.C., area. In the meantime he helps local Cambodians acquire English-language skills. Hong's story was featured in the* Refugee Voices Newsletter, *no. 34, in June 1995. Hong's contribution was written with the generous help of his former foster mother, Josephine Dunne, who is writing a book about Hong's life.*

# The Unplanned Journey

## HONG A. CHORK

I was born in a small village in Kampot Province, Cambodia, in 1968, the youngest of nine children. I have happy memories of my early childhood in this large family where everyone worked to grow our food. My father was a farmer and a very good carpenter. He was also very strict with us, and we often got a smack for being lazy or a smart ass, but we knew he worked hard for us. My mother spoiled me because I was the youngest, and I got away with a lot with her.

❀
123

I remember the smell of rice cooking in the morning fire, the rice fields, and the beautiful trees. I had a favorite water buffalo that I took to the fields. It was such a peaceful, quiet time. I knew nothing about politics, war, or material richness. I was a very happy village boy.

Everything changed when young Khmer Rouge soldiers dressed in black pajamas and carrying guns came to our village. I was six. They stayed with the villagers. Since they had guns, we listened to them and took care of them. We fed, clothed, and sheltered them. The land became communal. We stopped eating meals with our families. Instead, all the children had to eat together, and all the adults ate together. We weren't allowed to travel at night. The war was not far from us.

Some time later I noticed my mother looking sad. She

told me I had to "go away to school" with all the other young boys in the village. I remember the day the soldiers came for us in a big truck. I'll never forget this because one of them hit my little dog with his rifle and smashed its poor little head. Angry and depressed, I was thinking to myself that I would never want to be a soldier who did stupid things like that.

My innocence was taken away from me on that day. Until I returned to Cambodia from the United States in 1993, I didn't see my family (except for a brother) or my village again for almost twenty years!

The "school" far from my family was really a work farm. We were fed pretty well and lived in big sleeping rooms. I spent many hours every day working in the rice fields. We were told that Angka would care for us and our families and that we didn't need to miss our mothers.

After some time went by I was selected to go to the Phnom Penh leadership school. I was very proud of this because being a leader is what the Khmer Rouge talked about all the time. I was amazed by the city because I had never been far from my village. There were big buildings and noises.

The school was tough. I was disciplined a lot of the time. We had to wear student uniforms and had very long indoc-trination sessions. The soldiers taught us about Angka and the wrongs of capitalism. Angka was great. The revolution was great. We were going to be Angka's helpers in the war against evil.

During these sessions we had to accuse each other, even our friends, of doing bad things, like fighting. I learned that after being accused by my peers of something, the smart thing to do was to stand up right away, hang my head, and say to the Khmer Rouge soldiers, "I admit it." I did this even when statements made about me weren't true. The Khmer Rouge weren't interested in the truth; they got satisfaction in submission.

Because some other boys and I broke some of the rules,

we weren't going to be leaders. The Khmer Rouge kicked us out of school. I remember feeling bad. I knew nothing about what the Khmer Rouge were teaching, I just wanted to be smart and to do well.

They loaded us back on a truck and took us to the mountains, which was short for "you're on your own." We were taken to a barren place with a lot of old and sick people. We were on our own all right. We had no food. No shelter. We didn't know where we were or how to get anywhere. There was sickness and loneliness. I became very sick during this time, and my illness lasted for some months. It was due to all the trauma around me. I was away from my family. I had no food, no place to go. The Khmer Rouge didn't even want me.

People who were stuck in the same predicament fed me whatever food they could find, like wild berries and tree bark. They wet leaves and put them on my forehead to keep my fever down. From where we were we could see planes bombing the coast below the mountain. We all felt hopeless. "The Vietnamese have invaded Cambodia!" people said. "We must go to Thailand." We had to keep moving somewhere.

I didn't know what or where Thailand was. I walked and walked, hiding from Khmer Rouge soldiers and the Vietnamese. My feet were bloody from walking barefoot. I had no shoes. I traveled at night sometimes with a group, sometimes by myself, sometimes miles out of the way to avoid the fighting. There were gunshots fired close by at all times. Dead bodies were everywhere, including bodies of the military.

We met up with the Khmer Rouge from time to time. I was a small kid so no one handed me a gun to carry, but the Khmer Rouge asked me to carry munitions (I think they were grenades). Once I was carrying a bag of bombs to some Khmer Rouge soldiers when a bunch of Vietnamese guys came along and took them from me. I went back and got some more from the pile! Crazy kid.

There was a big mess when we reached the Thai border.

❀
125

Thai soldiers wouldn't let us cross, and the Khmer Rouge were there in our way. Amazingly, I recognized one of my older brothers, who was in the Khmer Rouge army. I wanted to stay with him because I was afraid and lonely. He told me to go to Thailand. "You will die if you stay here with me." I cried when he left me.

I was able to sneak across the border, and I brought food for the soldiers many times. This was dangerous, but plenty of kids did it. Finally, in about 1979, the United Nations or the Red Cross got us into the refugee camps in Thailand. I stayed with some Buddhist monks for a while. They were kind to me and even shaved my head so I would look like a Thai. I also lived with a Thai family for a while, and this is when I had a bad accident on a motorcycle. Because of the accident I returned to the camp. As an unaccompanied minor, I was asked by the relief agencies if I wanted to go to France or America. I chose America and moved to Washington, D.C.

Several foster homes later, after successful schooling and a spinal operation needed since my motorcycle accident, I went back to Cambodia. My last foster-care mother, who is also my best friend, took the trip with me. We went back during the Christmas–New Year's break from school.

The trip back awakened many memories. The sun beat strongly down on me. The roads to Kampot were paved with palm trees bending in the gentle breeze. In the distance were rice fields, and farther away were the familiar mountains. The anticipation of seeing my family again swelled inside me. When I saw my parents in my former village we hugged and cried. Sitting in the hut on stilts, I learned that of my siblings, two brothers and one sister are still alive. Five were killed by the Khmer Rouge.

I also was reminded of something that I learned after being thrown out of the Khmer Rouge school. I was very lucky to be from the village. Villagers were thought of as the old people. We were treated differently by the Khmer Rouge because we were peasants. The Khmer Rouge hated and were suspicious of the educated, savvy city people. Even though I was separated from my family for twenty years, I was spared a lot of pain. It was only after the Khmer Rouge brought me to the mountains to fend for myself did I see some of the pain that others suffered. I saw bodies, blood, and death along the roads. I saw mothers without children and kids like me who were alone. I heard a lot of chilling stories that didn't sound real.

My childhood was lost during those years. I will never be able to recapture this time. I will never be able to feel the peace that I did before I turned six. I will never be able to see my dead brothers and sisters again.

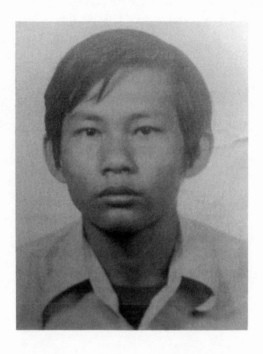

*VIBOLRETH BOU was eleven when the Khmer Rouge took over Cam-
bodia. He lost a brother to starvation. In 1979, Vibolreth arrived at the
Aranyaprathet Refugee Camp in Thailand. He was sponsored by Pastor
Hill of a Buffalo, New York, church. After graduating from high school
he attended the State University of New York at Cortland. He is married.
After being laid off at Congress, where he worked as a clerk, he began
studying to be a technician.*

❀  ❀  ❀

# *Motherland*

### VIBOLRETH BOU

*A lady walked toward me from the distance. Before she passed me, she asked, "Where are you going?" "I'm going to see people dancing in the village." The lady yielded a bit, turned half-way and smiled at me. As she walked by, her black hair waved through the wind like an angel. An old person in town told me a story that once upon a time there was a group of angels that came down from heaven, took off their wings and bathed in a lily pond. A man sneaked behind the bush, took an angel's wings, and frightened the rest of the angels away. The man and angel fell in love and lived happily ever after.*

Cambodia was once the land of pride and sanctity. As I walked through the countryside, the scenery overwhelmed me with tranquility and peace. Winds breathed upon the rice fields as waves in the ocean. Birds sang and sounds echoed through bamboo hedges that surrounded the lily pond. As a young boy I loved the tropical season and the monsoon rain. I still remember particular aromas and scenes of Cambodia before it turned into the horrid domain of the devil. In Cambodia I saw enough hell to last a life-time.

We were summoned by Khmer Rouge soldiers (whom

the world considers a Communist group but my mother calls "Maoist killers"). One of these devils stood up in front of us and shouted in a loud voice. He became so excited as he gestured with his arms and hands and as he walked back and forth. When he would spit out a word, a vein in his neck would bulge. Every sentence he spoke he would repeat: "We are free at last . . . at last from tycoons and feudalism. We have liberty and justice, liberty and justice. All people are equal. No one will be rich and no one will be poor. We have destroyed a fictitious belief. It is nonsense, such as God! God!"

My mother stood up immediately while her tears dripped down her cheeks to her lips. She looked straight at the Communist leader and said in an angry voice, "What kind of freedom do we have right now? Do you know what freedom means, comrade? Killing people every day is liberty and justice? Please, comrade, tell me! You live as a king and we live as slaves. Is this equal? Do these people here have anything to do with tycoons when they are starving to death?" Everyone was silent. Some people were stunned. One woman, who was carrying an AK–47 and wearing black pajamas, smirked. I had never seen my mother cry, nor had I noticed unhappiness from her before.

The next day, my brothers and I didn't see my mother return from work. One of our neighbors told us that she had gone far away. "Your mom will not come back," the comrade neighbor whispered while she looked around nervously. Before she could explain the disappearance of my mother, two well–armed men approached us and she walked away quickly.

One man told us that my mother was waiting for us in the other village. She was sent by Angka to attend an important meeting, since she was an intellectual and Angka now needed a person like her. "Don't you worry. Your mom is in great care. Our society needs people like her to support

Angka. Come! You all will be living in the other village," one of the Khmer Rouge said with enthusiasm while he patted my shoulder and looked at my brothers. Another armed man stood still calmly without saying a word. Both men were wearing black pajamas and carrying sacks of bullet magazines on their chests. They had mud stains up to their knees.

As both men escorted my three brothers and me away from the village, I could hear the machine gun growling and see human bodies of different ages lying on the flooded ground. Blood was everywhere. Blood was oozing from bodies even though they were motionless. My heart began to beat louder and harder when I saw my mother and others kneeling down with their arms tied behind their backs, elbow to elbow.

As I felt death approach us, two armed men appeared. The Khmer Rouge leader began to introduce the victims to the other two men, "This one is the police officer, this one is a doctor, and that one is the teacher," as he pointed to my mother, who was the last person. The doctor then appealed to the leader, "Please, comrade, please. What are the crimes? I've done nothing wrong. I'm only a doctor." The leader smirked and then said, "How do you bourgeoisie feel now? Where were you when we were suffering, living in the jungle, fighting the Americans and their puppet regime? You were home sleeping with wives on comfortable beds and making a mockery of us who were trying to liberate our country from French, Japanese, and American imperialism. We didn't then, and we certainly don't need you now. To keep you is no benefit and to destroy you is no loss."

Everyone was silent. Mother squinted her eyes, looking toward one of the two Khmer Rouge who had just arrived. "Is it you, Sok?" The Khmer Rouge looked at Mother. She was his former teacher. He was shocked, and then he turned

131

away quickly, as if he hadn't heard her. The leader raised his
rifle up to his right shoulder. Suddenly, smoke was expelled
from the muzzle while the butt of his rifle shook his shoulder. The sound of the gunfire appeared to shake the ground.
"Bang! Bang! Bang." The doctor was floundering to keep his
balance, but it was useless. His feet slipped and he fell down
into the dirt. His face no longer looked like that of a person.
Blood oozed from his skull, which had cracked open. A few
people screamed. One lady yelled toward the Khmer Rouge,
"Go to hell! You're devils."

While the appalling screams and groans of the people
were heard, the sounds of machine guns were rising like
thunder. Drizzling rain gently fell from heaven, as though a
goddess was crying for mercy. Lightning struck across the
sky above. Muddy clay on the soil and blood combined as
pus flowed across the victims' footprints. So much blood
that it flowed as though it was a stream.

My entire body began to feel agitated. I began to feel cold
and started calling my mother, "Mom!" My mother looked
at me without saying a word, then turned away toward the
sky and prayed, "Please, God, I do not ask you to feel sympathy toward me because I am crying but toward those I am
crying for." At that moment, the sound of a gun blasted into
my ears, "Bang! Bang! Bang!" One of the Khmer Rouge fell
to the ground. The Khmer Rouge leader screamed out just
before his neck burst open, "You traitor, Sok!" I looked to my
right. I saw one of the Khmer Rouge still alive, standing and
holding his rifle pointed toward the dead men. He looked at
my mother and in a croaking voice as he swallowed his tears
said to her, "I'm wrong. You are the only one that makes me
be a human."

My mother spoke to him after she had struggled to her
feet. "Now do you know what freedom means?" He firmly
responded, "Yes, freedom is what we must be willing to fight
and die for." My mother continued, "Yes, freedom does not

come free. Don't expect someone to come along to give you freedom, because they will likely destroy you or corrupt you rather than free you." The Khmer Rouge walked closer to my mother, cut the rope, freed her arms, and begged her, "Please forgive me."

*ARN YAN first lived in Rithy Sen camp and then Khao-I-Dang after the Khmer Rouge regime ended. In 1988 he was sponsored by his older brother. Arn now is an outreach worker with the United Cambodian Association of Minnesota. His involvement with Cambodian youth who are highly involved in crime brings him great fulfillment.*

———————————

# My Mother's Courage

### ARN YAN

During the 1970s, a great tragedy happened to the Cambodian people. I can remember this now, and I will not forget it for the rest of my life. In 1975 there was intense fighting between the government soldiers and the Khmer Rouge guerrillas. The Khmer Rouge took power. Everybody was extremely happy to get the new government. They hoped that they would have more freedom, liberty, and peace. But all they had been hoping for was gone.

My father had hoped that our family would stay together and that there would be no more killing. But only fifteen days after the Khmer Rouge took control of Cambodia, my father was accused by a cadre of being a former soldier or colonel of Lon Nol. He was really a cattle dealer between provinces. Before they killed him, they played a game with him. The killers let him eat all he wanted and then called him up to a small room and interrogated him about military matters. He knew nothing about these matters. He had never joined the army. When he didn't answer them, they hit and punished him by covering his head with a plastic bag and putting his head upside down in a jar full of water so that he lost consciousness several times.

After three days of interrogation, the man who called himself the King of Death made the decision to have my father killed. At that time, the faces of fifteen of the victims were covered with a dark cloth. One of the killers started telling those people to get on the truck. Everybody knew that they were going to be killed soon, but all they could do was plead with the murderers. Even though they all tried their best to beg not to be killed, their efforts were worthless.

When they arrived at the killing field, their faces looked pale. The killers told these innocent people to get off the truck and stand near the curb of Highway 5. Then they started counting "1 . . . 2 . . . 3 . . . ," and told them to run down to the field as they counted. The killers pointed their rifles at each of them and pulled the triggers. That was the end of my father's life. He was killed when he was forty-five years old. My mother has been a widow since.

Ten days after he died my mother went to ask one of the cadres about my father, "You told me that my husband would be coming back this week but it has been three weeks already." The man answered, "You don't have to worry about those betrayers. They will be coming back next week. They are so busy with their work. Don't ask me anymore about your husband." When my mother heard this she knew that my father had been killed. At that time I was about seven years old and I wondered why she didn't eat but just cried. I asked her, "What is the matter with you?" She answered by smiling with tears dripping from her face.

Three weeks passed by. My father didn't come back. I started asking my mother, "Where is Dad, Mom?" She didn't say anything to me. She just covered her face with a handkerchief and cried. When I saw that she was crying, I began to cry too. The next day she woke up early in the morning and went to the killer's office. When she arrived one of the killers came up and started asking her, "What did you come here for?" She answered, "I just want to know about my husband. You told me he would be coming, but now it has been five weeks already."

The man answered, "What! That's not your problem. That's your husband's problem. You don't have to know about those kinds of things." She knew that he was dead so she replied, "Why don't you send me to where my husband is staying?" The man turned to the group of people standing around and said, "If anybody is related to the men that aren't here, please come over to me." The rest of the people were told to go back home. There were about fifty people left, including my family.

Meanwhile, one killer stood up and spoke directly, "Please don't ask anymore about all those people who went to help Angka two months ago. You know they were betray- ers and they were former Lon Nol soldiers. They all were sent to death." In the meantime, all the victims' relatives cried, shouted, and yelled at that stupid man. "How come you killed my husband! He wasn't a soldier. He was a rice farmer." The Khmer Rouge cadre announced, "If anyone wants to know some more about their husbands, come to my office tomor- row night." A lot of people went back, but my family didn't. We were afraid of being killed. We later learned that the peo- ple who did go back to the cadre were killed.

In June 1975, I was called to work as a grass carrier. I worked seven days a week from six o'clock in the morning till noon. They gave us about a twenty-minute break during lunchtime. We worked again from twelve-twenty until six in the evening. All the children from six to ten years old had to go to work. They divided us into groups according to age. I some- times worked fourteen hours per day. That was hard for me.

During 1975, the first year of the Khmer Rouge control, we had enough food to eat. But from 1976 to 1978 we didn't have enough food to eat and we weren't allowed to cook for ourselves. They had to cook for us and we had to eat together in groups of ten to fifteen people. Sometimes I didn't get my ration because I didn't finish my work on time and my food was thrown away. We ate gruel, rice mixed up with a banana stump, and one can of rice was put into the big pot. That one can of rice fed one hundred children, and we could hardly find a grain on the plate. All that we could find was the stump of banana. This didn't make us healthy. After we ate, we got sick a lot from diarrhea, cholera, and stomachaches. Day by day, hundreds of children and adults died from starvation, and this was just in the small village where I lived.

One day I was very sick and starving to death. I didn't go to work. I just stayed in the children's cottage. One of my group leaders came up to me and spoke in a loud voice, "Why don't you go to work?" I responded, "I am sorry. I can't go to work." He asked me again, "What's the matter with you?" I answered, "I'm sick. I'm hungry. I don't have any strength in my body at all. Please forgive me, sir!" I said this kneeling down on the ground with my two hands held up to him. I hadn't finished what I was saying when he picked me up. He smacked and kicked me until I dropped to the ground. I lost consciousness for a couple of hours.

When I woke up, my face and body were covered with blood. I could hardly walk, and I was very scrawny because I hadn't eaten food for two days. I was sent to the hospital to be treated. In the hospital they didn't have any real medicine. All they had were fake medicines and traditional medicines made from tree leaves, stumps, and roots. Some traditional medicine could help us, but others didn't have any effect. None of the medications helped me.

One week later my mother heard that I was in the hospital. She was shocked. She came to visit me but she didn't recognize me because I was very, very skinny. The moment she saw me she cried and said to me, "What can I do for you? I don't have anything left besides my body." She came to visit me every day and packed some kind of food for me whenever she came. She got some medicine for me by exchanging valuable things like diamonds, gold, necklaces, earrings, and bracelets that she had hidden in the ground around our hut. She came to visit me by stealing time from her work. If the soldiers had known, she would have been in big trouble. After I got some medicine from her, I started to feel a little bit better. When I felt back to normal I was called to work in the children's team again.

One year later, in 1976, I was sent to another province to work on transplanting rice, pulling out rice seedlings, and carrying bunches of rice. That was the hardest year in my village. People went to work every day and worked really hard in the fields but they didn't get enough food to survive. All the crops that they grew were sent to China.

Sometimes I was out of rations, so I had to go out and steal all kinds of vegetables and fruit, such as potatoes, papayas, pumpkins, and watermelons. They were planted at the place where many people were buried in shallow graves. I went out almost every night to steal with my friends. I remember one rainy night when all the people around me were sleeping, and I asked one of my friends, "Do you want to go to steal with me?" He said, "No! Are you crazy?"

Nobody wanted to go because it was very dangerous and quiet there. Wild animals like wolves, snakes, monkeys, and tigers lived there. When I went, there was only the sound of these animals. Even though I was very scared and knew I would be killed if I was caught, I was determined to eat. Nothing is worse than starving. I didn't care about being arrested and being killed. That night I was so filled up that I couldn't walk or go back to the work camp. When the sun rose I woke up and walked straight to work. One of my group leaders came up to me and asked, "Where were you last night?" I told him that I had gone to my mother's house. He didn't hit me this time, but I was punished by being put to work for twenty-four hours in the field. Everybody went home except me, but luckily I finished all the work he required me to do.

139

The year 1977 was the worst year for people in Battambang province. They grew a lot of rice, but there was a big flood that destroyed all the crops that had already been planted. There was nothing left in the fields but water, seedlings, and straw. Day after day, we had almost nothing to eat. There was no rice or vegetables. We had some cassava, stump of papaya, lilies, and fish to sustain us. In 1975 they had required at least seven to ten people to live in one hut. A few years later there was nobody in those small houses anymore. In one house, at least five people died, and in some houses there was nobody left. They were killed, and others died from starvation, disease, and lack of medication. At the hospital no one was educated, so most of the time sick people weren't helped. The Khmer Rouge killed the doctors, professors, teachers, lawyers, and high-ranking people.

One thousand Cambodians were left in my village. About six thousand had died. The village was so quiet. In some huts everybody had died and nobody buried them. The bad smell spread all over the village. Sometimes I drank water with a bad smell and with blood floating in it. Nobody could do anything for anyone else even if they were friends or close family members. All they could do was to survive by getting food to eat.

Early in 1978 one of my cousins was killed because he made a small mistake. In the morning he went to work plowing and raking the field. He saw a fish swimming in the water. He stepped down from the plow to catch the fish and put it in his pocket. One of the Khmer Rouge leaders was watching from behind him. He dragged my cousin down from the plow, telling him, "You're supposed to come to work. You're not supposed to come to catch fish." The man hit my cousin on his head and neck with a bamboo stick until he died.

When they put you to work, you worked. They had somebody follow you all the time, keeping an eye on you every second. Before that man hit my cousin, my cousin said, "Please forgive me, sir. Please don't hit me. I won't do it again." At the time, I was carrying rice seedlings to transplant in the field. I didn't know my cousin was being beaten and killed. I thought it was somebody else. After he was killed with the bamboo stick, one of my friends came up and whispered, "Arn, do you know what happened to your cousin?" I said I didn't know. "Arn, if I tell you, don't get surprised, okay?" He told me that the man they put on the dike who was hit and died was my cousin. I said, "What? The man with the bloody body on the dike, he was my cousin?" He answered, "Yes."

When I saw that he was lying in the field, I was so depressed, and I asked myself what he did wrong. I could do nothing besides feel very sorry for him, bless him to go to heaven, and hope that God takes care of him. From then on, every second we were working the killers always came behind us. They wouldn't let people go to work from one place to another. If we wanted to work somewhere else, we had to ask them. If we didn't ask, we would be in big trouble. They punished us by sending us to jail or by killing us. Their doctrine gave us no human rights, no sympathy, and no freedom to do anything. Sometimes we made only a small mistake but they pointed us out to the killers and we would be killed.

The Khmer Rouge tortured and killed people in many different ways. They sometimes pushed people's heads into a barrel full of water. Sometimes they pulled out the fingernails. Other times they dug three holes in a triangle shape and buried all of the people's bodies except for the heads. Then they put a pot on the heads and burned a fire until the people died. Sometimes they put people in a pot covered with a lid and built a fire.

Many times they killed people by cutting out their livers with a knife. They buried the bodies but used the livers and gallbladders to make traditional medicine for fevers. Often they ate the livers. Sometimes they hanged people, and sometimes they covered their heads with plastic bags. Babies were thrown up in the air and came down on bayonets. Other times they grabbed babies' feet and hit them on tree stumps.

I survived the Khmer Rouge largely because my mother really cared about me. She stole rice and vegetables. When she knew I had stolen something, she told me not to do it again. She said, "I am old and I will be dead someday. I don't want you to die." Even though she stole every day, there still wasn't enough for us to eat. Luckily, we are alive today, and we lost only my father and my brother. But for the rest of my life I will not forget these unimaginable, tragic events that have happened to me.

*SOPHANARITH "RITH" MEAN (with family) and his family were sponsored in November 1975 by an American family. One month after leaving Khao-I-Dang refugee camp, they arrived in Colorado Springs, Colorado, where they still live. Rith plans to finish college. His main focus will be wellness management, and he plans to work in a health-related field.*

❀ ❀ ❀

# *Escaping the Horror*

**RITH MEAN**

$M$y family was one of the lucky ones to have survived the killing fields of Cambodia. Over 1 million Cambodians were not so lucky–they suffered from starvation and died from being tortured or were executed.

On April 17, 1975, during the Cambodian New Year, Phnom Penh was overtaken by Pol Pot and the Khmer Rouge. The Khmer Rouge forced fellow Cambodians to evacuate the city and march to the countryside. Those who survived the ordeal were forced to work in labor camps for almost four years.

On April 17, 1975, my family was fortunate enough to be living in Pailin, a city that is only a few miles away from the Thai–Cambodian border. News of the fall of Phnom Penh was slow to arrive, but we knew that there was something peculiar going on. My father worked as a border patrolman, and he had some indication that the government in Phnom Penh was going to be destroyed.

My family was a large one, not uncommon for Cambodian families. There was my father, Phan Mean, and my mother, Vann Mean, who was pregnant at the time. The four boys in the family were Rassy, Sophanarith (me), Sophanara, and Sophanaro. The three girls were Vanthavy, Sophear, and Preakdey.

That afternoon I was out playing with my friends. For

some reason I felt that I needed to go home. When I arrived, my entire family was loaded into a jeep ready to take off for the Thai border. They couldn't find me so their plan was to return for me later that night. They couldn't wait any longer because the Khmer Rouge were on their way! Fortunately, I made it home and all of us were headed to Thailand.

It was too late, though. The Khmer Rogue were ahead of us, and they had the roads blockaded. They were young boys, not much older than me. I was nine years old. They had hatred in their eyes and vengeance in their voices. Among the Khmer Rouge boys was one older man.

The man recognized my father because they had met before when my father was patrolling the border. My father pleaded with the man to let his family go through the blockade because his children were all so young. He wanted to get us safely to Thailand. My father was very sick at this time.

The man persuaded the young Khmer Rouge soldiers to let my family pass, but we had to bribe them with the few valuable possessions we had with us. In our haste to leave Pailin, we had packed only some gold and jewelry, which we gave to the Khmer Rouge. Everything else was left behind.

There was a rickety bridge over a river that separated Cambodia from Thailand. For us, reaching the other side meant salvation from devastation. I still can hear the gunshots aimed at our jeep as we crossed that bridge. I don't know if the Khmer Rouge let us pass because they pitied us or if they did it as a game to taunt us. We did make it safely to Thailand.

In Thailand we stayed at camp Khao–I–Dang. At first, things were going well there. We had food, shelter, and clothing–the basics. But the longer we stayed at the camp, the rougher things began to get. The food that was supposed to be distributed to us was withheld by some of the Thai guards. It was as if we had worn out our welcome in Thailand and they were becoming irritated with us. My mother cooked food and sold it on the streets to get extra money.

My younger brothers and I went to work in the cornfields. Our job was to remove corn kernels from the cob by hand.

My oldest brother, Rassy, was one of the active individuals in the camp. He knew that the Thai guards were holding back food, so he and a couple of other people protested. During that protest the Thai guards started shooting Cambodians, killing many.

My younger brother, Sophanara, was one of the people to die. He was shot in the head. My family was devastated. There were only a few days left before we were to come to the United States. So why him? At eight years old, he never had a chance to see the world. We had his body cremated and could only leave his ashes in a church in Thailand.

Many missionaries came through the camps when we stayed there and influenced Rassy to convert to Christianity. His new belief and the connections he made talking to the missionaries helped our family get sponsored by a Christian couple. On November 29, 1975, our paperwork was processed and we were on our way to the United States of America.

We took a U.S. military airplane from Bangkok, Thailand. We flew over many different countries, but I remember flying over the state of Alaska. It was very cold looking, and it was the first time any of us had seen snow. We landed in Fort Chaffee, a refugee camp, and stayed there about two weeks. We had finally made it!

On December 12, 1975, we landed in Colorado Springs, Colorado, and have made this our home ever since. My father committed suicide in 1981. He hanged himself. We are now a family of eight. We made it out of Cambodia without ever experiencing the killing fields. Sometimes when things are getting rough for me and I want to give up, I think back to the time when I could have been left behind in Pailin. What would have happened to me if I hadn't rushed home that day?

*CHANRITHY HIM's parents were killed by the Khmer Rouge, and three of her siblings died during their reign. She lived in refugee camps in Thailand and the Philippines for two years after the Khmer Rouge reign ended. On November 14, 1981, she was sponsored to come to the United States by her uncle, Leng Seng. Chanrithy now lives in Eugene, Oregon, where she received her bachelor of science degree in biochemistry from the University of Oregon. She is applying to medical schools to fulfill her childhood dream of becoming a doctor. Chanrithy is completing her book* When Broken Glass Floats, *which describes her ordeal during the Khmer Rouge regime. She also works part time for the Department of Child Psychiatry at Oregon Health Sciences University, which is conducting a twelve-year follow-up study of former Cambodians who survived the Khmer Rouge. Since 1983, Chanrithy has been performing Cambodian traditional dances.*

✿  ✿  ✿

# When the Owl Cries

**CHANRITHY HIM**

$A$t the labor camp where we lived when I was eleven, I
planted rice in the muddy fields. One day I cut myself when
I stepped on a tree branch buried in the deep mud. I
screamed, "Ow! I cut myself. Ow! It hurts." I reached for the
branch and took it to dry land so nobody else would step on
it. I felt the pain and looked at my foot. It was bleeding. I
wiped the gray–black mud off my foot and the blood flowed
out steadily.

I wanted to cry but I was afraid of the Khmer Rouge. I
never knew what they might do to me. I looked at the cut
and didn't want to go in the mud again because it would
make my foot infected. However, I knew that I must work in
the mud, planting rice with the women and children in
order to avoid accusation or punishment.

My foot gradually became infected. It got worse every
day because I had to walk a long way through the woods to
the field and back to the hut. Also, there was no proper
medicine, except for hot water to clean the wound. I thought
the infection might kill me.

My mother had to work every day for the Khmer Rouge and take care of my siblings and me after she came back, exhausted. She didn't have time to find the sour leaves for me to boil in order to get the juice to clean my wound. My left foot was itchy and painful. I laid it on the bamboo on which I slept. It felt hot around the wound, and the rest of my body felt hot too. The pain ached from my foot to my waist. It was almost like something was pinching me hard. The pain was so unbearable that every night I kept banging my foot and hands against the bamboo floor. I tore palm leaves off the walls. I tried to sleep to forget it, thrashing around, trying to cope with the excruciating pain, but it never went away.

I cried and screamed very hard during the quiet nights. I thought people in the village heard me because the huts were built very close to each other. When it became unbearable, I would call to my mother, "Mak, please help me, please help me." Sometimes she came and scratched softly around the wound to ease the pain. I would go back to sleep for a while, but the pain would wake me up. For about one or two weeks, I cried every night. My mother was getting sick because my crying kept her awake. I kept calling for her to come and scratch around my wound to ease my pain. She came to help me many times, but when she was too tired, she had to go back to sleep.

There was an old lady whose hut was behind ours. One night she woke my mother up and told her, "Why don't you take care of your daughter? She's crying all night." In frustration, my mother said, "I'm helping her but can't help my daughter enough. I'm exhausted."

One morning I decided to find sour leaves by myself. I could not walk, so I crawled from the village past a grove of mango trees to a place where they buried people. Nearby there was a small path where the ox carts traveled. I crawled on the path past guava and bamboo trees, searching for sour leaves to clean my wound.

I crawled for an hour until I got to a yucca plant field. I crawled around, trying to find sour leaves, and finally I saw some big ones on the other side of a thorn fence. I tried to get to them but couldn't because of the thorns, until I saw a small hole in the fence which I crawled through and into the field.

While I was picking sour leaves, a tall man came up behind me. He was dressed in black and carried a long, curved knife. He said, "Comrade, what are you doing? Are you stealing?" "No, I'm not stealing. I'm only picking sour leaves," I softly replied. I was frightened. He grabbed me and began dragging me to a tree.

"Please don't hurt me," I begged. He didn't say anything and kept dragging me, pulling me by the arm around the yucca field to the tree. I was crying and telling him that I wasn't stealing. He yanked my old torn scarf from around my neck and threw it on the ground. I was sure he saw the sour leaves that spilled out. I wondered, *why is he so cruel to me?* He tied my arms behind my back tightly from the wrist to elbow and pushed me down on my knees. He then tied the rope to the tree.

"I will kill you at sunset," he said. I implored him again and again, "Please, don't kill me. Don't kill me, please. I wasn't stealing. I was just picking sour leaves to clean my swollen foot. I'm telling you the truth, so please spare my life." I cried out in fear. "Don't lie, comrade." In a forceful voice the man in black said, "I don't believe what you say. I will kill you. Say no more." I softly cried, "If you don't believe me, just look at my infected wound. I don't lie. I need these leaves for my foot because it is painful. Please, spare my life. Please, don't kill me."

While I was beseeching him, I wished I were in a position to respectfully bow down to him, which might lead him to

❀
149

forgive me. It was too late. I was already tied to the tree. My imploring didn't persuade the man. He went away, disappearing into the grove of trees behind me. He carried a long, sharp knife on his right shoulder. He shouted, "I will cut off your head at sunset so that the people coming home from working in the woods can see you. Then they won't follow your bad example." I heard his feet stepping on the dry leaves.

I looked at the sour leaves on the ground and kept thinking how little things got me into trouble. I kept wondering why he accused me of stealing. I looked at the hole in the fence where I got through and thought if people had put more thorns to make the fence then I wouldn't have gotten in.

I grew scared as I thought about dying. I cried hard and loud. Many tears fell until, as time passed, my sobbing became softer and softer. I was exhausted and bound so tightly that I never thought of escaping.

In the late afternoon, I heard birds in the trees. When I heard them, I cried, thinking of the owl. Many people in Cambodia believe that when the owl cries, it is going to take someone's life. When I heard the birds, I thought, *Maybe this is my time to die. At sunset the owl will cry and take my life after the man has killed me.*

The pain in my left foot and leg increased because I was kneeling on both legs. I struggled to put weight on my right leg to help alleviate the pressure on my wound. *I am going to die soon,* I kept thinking. As I cried, I thought about my mother. I pondered, *How will she know what happened to me if the man kills me? Maybe people will see my dead body and tell her. Maybe the Khmer Rouge are going to throw my body away, and she won't find out what happened to me. How sad will she be? How will she endure not knowing what has happened? Will she blame herself because she didn't help me?*

As I asked myself those questions, I cried and cried out of frustration. I wished the wind could take my message to my mother, telling her, *I'm in trouble.* At least then she would know what had happened to me.

I was so sad. I imagined how painful my death would be. The tears rushed down my bony cheeks and into my mouth. I thought, *I'm not ready to die yet.*

I was tied to the tree from morning to sunset. I imagined people coming home from clearing the woods. I would be embarrassed and ashamed to let them see me tied to the tree. I was afraid that these people would talk to my mother and tell her that I was stealing, without knowing the truth. At the same time, I thought they would feel sorry for me because I would die soon.

I imagined the man raising the big, long knife in the air and swinging it down toward my neck. I cried and cried. I shut my eyes and lowered my head and asked, *Why would anybody be so cruel to a little child like me who is helpless and struggling to live?*

When the sun set all the way behind me, it got dark and I thought that my time had come. I prayed to God and called for my father's spirit and my oldest sister's spirit to help me when I thought about death. Again, I imagined the man coming to kill me. His rapid footsteps would echo behind me and before I could take another breath, he'd kill me. I was shaking, terrified. My mouth was dry. My face and neck felt sticky because I had been crying all day. I was also exhausted and hungry, and finally my crying became softer.

Suddenly I heard his footsteps and dropped my last tears. I was terrified, shaking and cold. I looked down to the ground and shut my eyes. I tightened my body to control the instant pain, not knowing whether I should scream or bite my lip. When he came close, I got ready to die.

All of a sudden, I heard the sound of rope cutting behind my back, which terrified me. Soon I felt my tied arms swing free, released from the trunk of the tree. I opened my eyes instantly and tried to think about what was going on behind me. I turned back and looked. The man in black said, "Comrade, now I set you free. Don't do that again."

Then he untied the rough rope from my numb wrists. In tears, I was extremely happy and enormous energy surged through me. I grabbed my torn scarf and put it around my neck, leaving the sour leaves on the ground behind me. I struggled to get up and walk, but I couldn't. With the unimaginable excitement of being set free, I had forgotten that I couldn't walk. I crawled as fast as I could through the hole in the fence without turning back.

The birds cried in the woods. It was as if they were singing songs to celebrate my release. I struggled down to the deeply carved ox path and slowly struggled up the other side. I pulled myself up by grabbing onto the plants along the bank. While I was crawling, I just couldn't believe that I had been released. It seemed like a dream. At the same time, the voice of the man and his words stuck in my mind. "Comrade, now I set you free. Don't do that again."

The joy of survival was in my heart as I crawled past the grove of trees toward the community of huts where we lived. As I approached ours, I looked at every detail. I couldn't believe that I had returned to our hut. It seemed like a close friend that I missed so much. "Oh, my hut. Oh, my hut," I cried.

I dragged my left foot along the ground, crawling toward the hut. When I saw my beloved mother inside, I was so happy. It seemed impossible. I told her how the man was going to kill me. Her eyes filled with tears that rolled down her cheeks. I cried too, and she took a scarf and wiped my tears.

"Oh, Mak, I thought I wouldn't see you again . . ." I kept

crying. She stroked my hair. "You're lucky. I'm so glad that you weren't killed," she said. Her tear-filled eyes looked directly toward me in an expression of sorrow. Then she reached out to hold me as if she would never let go.

SEATH K. TENG (and family) lost a sister and a brother to starvation under the Khmer Rouge. In 1979 her family left Cambodia to seek refuge at Khao-I-Dang refugee camp along Thailand's border. In 1982 they were sponsored by Blessed Sacrament Catholic Church in Lawton, Oklahoma, and came to America. She now lives in Modesto, California, where she attends nursing school and works part time as a student nurse. She will graduate in fall 1996.

❀  ❀  ❀

# The End of Childhood

**SEATH K. TENG**

Come with me. I'll take you to the village to play with all the other children, and before dark, someone will take you back to your mom." This alluring statement changed my life as a child for almost three years. The time that I started to realize and become interested in the world was when I faced the most hateful things in life. At the age of four I was robbed of my normal childhood. I was separated from my family to face the cruelty and hatred of the Khmer Rouge.

My family was separated from each other to work in different places. Until the end of 1975 we were able to live with our mother. One morning, while my mother, sister and I were pulling weeds at the watermelon farm, we saw two Khmer Rouge soldiers approach us. They came to take my sister to the village. I wanted to be with her. I had never been away from her, so the two soldiers took both of us. They said that we could come home any time we wanted. But this wasn't the case at all.

When we got to the village there were many children already there not much older than me. I saw my grandmother and my aunt. I ran to them but one soldier pulled me back, telling me to be still. I cried, throwing both my arms at my grandmother and aunt to take me, but they didn't come. The feeling of rejection was burning inside me. I thought that both my grandmother and aunt didn't love me. All I could think about was my mom, and being away from her made me cry more and more. I was fortunate at that time because I had my sister. She was my only comfort until they took her away from me.

After the Khmer Rouge got all of the children, they took us to long shacks made of bamboo with a roof made of palm leaves. In the middle was an open area where all the meetings were held. Before they assigned us a place to sleep, they held a long meeting. We all sat in the open square listening to the loud intercom. The Khmer Rouge soldiers told us not to love our parents or to depend on them because they are not the ones who supported us. They told us to love the new leaders and to work hard so that our country could be prosperous. If we didn't do as they said, we would get a severe beating for punishment. After the meeting they made us cheer and keep repeating that we love, work hard for and respect our new government.

They then took us to sleep in the long shelter. They made us sleep in a row. In one shelter there were two rows of children sleeping with their feet facing each other. We slept on a bamboo floor with no sheets, no cover or pillow. The Khmer Rouge soldiers slept in their hammocks high above us.

Early in the morning, before sunlight, they shouted and whistled for us to get up and get in line to go to work. We were very tired, and some of us didn't get up on time. If we didn't get up they would pull us up on our feet and threaten to beat us if we were slow again. Every morning before sunlight we all went to work without anything to eat. We did a variety of work depending on the jobs that needed to be done.

I remember that we did most of the jobs in the rice field. We grew so much rice, but they fed us so little. What we did depended on the season. The adults did all the planting. What little piece of the rice plants the adults dropped, we had to gather and give them back to plant. To do this we had to stay in muddy water all day. The only time we came out of the muddy water was around noontime, when it was time to eat our first meal. We only had one set of clothing. We slept in it wet or dry.

In the harvesting season we picked up the rice strands that the adults dropped when the plant was cut. This time of the year was hard for us because the rice field was very dry and the rice stubs cut our bare feet. This physical pain to our feet we could endure. The most terrible pain we had to endure was hunger pain. Our meals were always rice porridge with salt. The Khmer Rouge soldiers fed us only two meals a day. They gave us one bowl for every four children. As Charles Darwin put it, it was survival of the fittest. Whoever could eat the fastest got more to eat. They didn't give us a spoon, either. We just used our hands.

Besides working in the rice field, the children pulled weeds from the vegetable garden. Sometimes the Khmer Rouge took us to the mountain to collect rocks for building bridges. If we didn't do our job we would get a beating and not be allowed to eat our meals. To eat, we had to work hard. If we were really sick and couldn't work that day, we were allowed to eat only one meal with extra liquid in our rice porridge. They said we didn't provide any labor and that we were lucky to eat for free.

157

We worked seven days a week without a break. The only time we got off work was to see someone get killed, which served as an example for us. Eighteen years have passed, and I can still remember one of these killings vividly. Sometimes I have nightmares about it. I remember a day we were working in the vegetable garden pulling weeds. In the middle of working, the whistle blew and the soldiers told us to stop. They said we had to go to a meeting to see the punishment of a traitor. When we got there they made us sit in front near the victim so we could get a close look at what was going to happen.

In the center of the meeting place was one woman who had both of her hands tied behind her. She was pregnant and her stomach bulged out. Before her stood a little boy who was about six years old and holding an ax. In his shrill voice, he yelled for us to look at what he was going to do. He said that if we didn't look, we would be the next to be killed. I guess we all looked, because the woman was the only one killed that day. The little boy was like a demon from hell. His eyes were red and he didn't look human at all. He used the back of his ax and slammed it hard on the poor woman's body until she dropped to the ground. He kept beating her until he was too tired to continue.

We were taught not to love or respect anybody besides the Khmer Rouge government. If we were caught hugging or talking intimately to our parents, we would get a beating. I didn't get a beating for this because I never saw any of my family members. During the time I was at the children's workplace I never thought about my family. I was brainwashed from all the meetings we had to attend.

There were incidents of children running away from this place. They never succeeded. They were caught and brought back. Whenever that happened there would be a meeting, and one of the soldiers would tie up the runaway. After that the Khmer Rouge would point at the children. Whoever was pointed at had to do the beating. If we didn't participate or if we didn't beat severely enough, we would be the next victim and also be beaten. To save ourselves from being hit, we hit hard. After the beating they left the bloody kid there and starved him until they put him to work again. While these beatings took place they made us shout, saying they deserved it because they were traitors and were a bad example for everybody.

At the reeducation meetings, I believed the Khmer Rouge soldiers when they told us that our families did not love us. I kept in my mind the first time I was at the village, when I cried, wanting to go to my grandmother and aunt, and they didn't come to me. At the time, I didn't know that the Khmer Rouge government made us behave this way.

I was told later, toward the end of 1978, that we were free to leave the children's workplace. I had no idea where my family was and felt very lucky that my sister found me and took me to our parents. I was almost seven when I saw my parents for the first time since I was separated from them three years earlier.

DARITH KEO (far right) was sponsored in 1982 by relatives who had fled Cambodia before the takeover. He came to the United States from an international Red Cross refugee camp in Thailand. He now lives with his wife, Chhloey Horl, in Turlock, California, and works for the Modesto Bee as a reporter.

# My Sadness

## DARITH KEO

I saw my mother's tears glistening in the dim light of a
dying bonfire. A farm labor overseer had just ordered fifteen
children to kick me. I was seven. Each child was to kick me
five times, and my mother could do nothing to stop it.

My crime? I was absent from the twelve–hour–a–day
work in the rice paddies because of a fever brought on by an
ulcer the size of an Oreo cookie on my hip. The ulcer was the
product of working in the parasite–infested water of the rice
fields all day. My job was to clear branches and weeds from
the paddies. Sometimes I had to dig irrigation ditches with
a special shovel made for little hands.

I was ordered to stay silent, but after fifteen blows, I
looked up at the man. I was going to tell him that I was sick.
Before I could speak, the man ordered the remaining twelve
children to kick me eight times each, instead of five.

My ulcer then broke and bled after so many blows. My
mother's tears. Endless labor without pay. Hunger. Beatings.
Executions. These are the memories I have of my childhood
in Cambodia during the holocaust of the Khmer Rouge, from
1975 to 1979.

I was born in 1970 in Pailin and raised in Battambang. We
were city folk. Our neighborhood had about five hundred
people, mostly peasants and merchants. We were all related
or close friends.

My father died of a fever when I was two. My mother never remarried. When I was four years old, the Khmer Rouge were all around our community. B–52s would fly right above our roof. Then I would hear the explosions. We stayed at home during the bombings, sometimes huddling in a dry well behind the house. Sometimes the neighbors would join us. Outside, people would rush back and forth with children in their arms.

The commotion went on for months, but my house was never hit. When the Khmer Rouge took control of our area during the spring of 1975, they fired guns into the air and gave us less than two hours to pack our bags and head to the countryside. They announced that the Americans were on their way to bomb our cities.

During the evacuation Khmer Rouge soldiers sang their new national anthem and told us about the new socialist government, Angka, under the leadership of Pol Pot. Pol Pot was a name that had not been heard before by anyone I knew. Those who refused to leave their homes were accused of being pro–American and were beaten or shot to death.

We didn't have a clue what the Khmer Rouge were up to. Soon Pol Pot's government began mass executions. At first the Khmer Rouge was secretive about the killings because they didn't want to frighten people.

Khmer Rouge officers rounded up former soldiers and other officials of the Lon Nol government and took them away in jeeps and military trucks. The Khmer Rouge told them that Prince Norodom Sihanouk was returning and that they were to be part of the welcoming celebration. My grandmother's sister's family was taken away at this time. We never saw any of these people again.

Kids from five to twelve years old were placed in the child labor group. Those thirteen and older were taken away from their families to join the youth labor force. We had to work from sunup to sundown, and the older people worked even longer hours. Education was abandoned.

At night Khmer Rouge children in black pajamas and red scarves danced around a bonfire, waving wooden objects. We were allowed to join them, but sleep was more precious to me than trying to perform that scary dance. Pol Pot was trying to brainwash us.

Twice a day we ate watery rice. Sometimes they gave us a couple of pieces of rock salt as a side dish.

We were separated from my mother most of the time because she was sent to work at remote locations, either growing rice or building dams. Because she was a city person, my mother had a rough time dealing with the mud and leeches. Our grandparents took care of us when she was taken away.

My grandfather worked in the clinic. He knew how to heal using leaves, roots, and other natural sources. The Khmer Rouge didn't use modern medicine. The clinic was run by Khmer Rouge women who thought they had enough skills to be nurses. They learned medicine in three-month-long courses given by doctors who were scheduled for execution.

When we were separated from Mom, a rumor made it back to our camp that she was near death. I made some medicine with shells, roots, and minerals, imitating as best as I could what I had seen my grandfather do. I poured the solution into an empty bottle and stowed away on a supply wagon heading to her camp.

The ox-driven wagon arrived at night. People were surprised to see a seven-year-old at their camp, but they kept quiet about it. My mother was happy to see me. She cried, hugged me, and gave me all her night's ration of food.

She looked like an old lady to me, but she was only twenty-seven. I gave her the medicine and she took it right away. She said she could feel the coolness of the medicine going down her throat and felt relief from blisters that developed in her mouth. She told me it was like a magic potion.

We slept that night on the same hammock. I felt totally safe, like I was back home before the war. I left my mother at three in the morning, when she had to report to work. By now the driver had learned of his passenger and quietly agreed to take me back to the main work camp.

Each day as we toiled in rice fields we saw men and women with hands tied behind their backs being led away by soldiers. Each time I saw this my heart would race. Before my heartbeat could return to normal I would hear gunshots echoing in the background. Sometimes the soldiers were not so discreet. Once they made the people sit in a circle and watch as they executed an unmarried couple. They were clubbed on the neck and fell near a ditch. The Khmer Rouge henchmen pushed them into the hole with their shins. The couple went into spasms and were buried alive.

The Khmer Rouge arranged all marriages. Premarital af-fairs were considered a capital crime. There were many cap-ital crimes, including stealing food, being highly educated, or ever having worked for the old government.

My grandfather had a college degree and had been a for-est ranger. Only by concealing his identity was our family able to stay alive. The Khmer Rouge would have killed the entire family had they found out that a family member used to be somebody big.

They feared rebellion, and we feared them. A few people tried to escape, but they were caught and killed.

Even during these darkest days of captivity I clung to the good memories of my early childhood. They would help me make it through the day during the times of hard labor. I would remember the rustling of mango leaves in the back of our house. Taking a shower in the rain. How warm I felt inside when I came back in the house and my mom would wrap me in a blanket. My first day of preschool.

I also kept thinking about food. We always had enough to eat before the takeover. My grandmother picked mangoes and other fruits for me. My godfather took me to the local market and gave me coloring pencils, money, candy, and ice cream.

I kept hoping that things would go back to being the way they were. I really didn't understand what was going on. Four years seemed forever. The memories almost ran out.

In late 1978 we heard that the Cambodian freedom fighters were driving some Khmer Rouge forces deep into the jungle. When all the Khmer Rouge officers in our camp left for the battle, we grabbed what we could and headed back to the city. The freedom fighters were nowhere. Instead, there were thousands of Vietnamese soldiers.

We finally reached our home in Battambang. We found my house and my grandfather's house destroyed. The foundations were being used for threshing rice. We stayed there for six months after the Vietnamese liberation.

My mom began trading rice that we received from the Vietnamese for fabric, candy, combs, and other goods with Thai merchants along the border. She would sell her goods for more rice back in the cities. Rice became the currency. She was the only woman in a group of ten merchants doing the trading. They would travel to the border carrying their goods on bicycles. Mom's bicycle had no brakes. One time when the bandits robbed the group, she got away because she was loaded down and unable to stop. She worried that the bandits would shoot her but they didn't.

Later the Vietnamese stopped sending rice, instead supplying people with moldy corn that caused diarrhea. During that time we learned about camps being set up by the United Nations and the Red Cross along the Thai border for Cambodians seeking shelter. My mother decided that we should go there.

*DAVE LONH arrived in Thailand in 1982, and in 1983 he was spon-*
*sored by the YMCA in Texas and brought to the United States. His father*
*disappeared during the Khmer Rouge rule and is assumed to be dead.*
*Because of his age and sketchy knowledge of English, he was sent to an*
*adult high school, where he received his high school diploma. He now*
*attends the community college in Orange County, California, majoring in*
*electronics.*

❀  ❀  ❀

# *Life in Communism*

### DAVE LONH

**M**y memories never go away. I worked as a farmer, as many people in Cambodia did. Communist leaders demanded that children and the elderly work. We had to dig the ground and plant rice by hand. We produced much rice, but the Communist soldiers wouldn't give us enough to eat.

After work we had to find something else to fill our stomachs. We ate almost everything that we saw. I saw a few people eat their own pets. I ate a lot of creatures, such as mice, bats, and insects. We ate grass like animals.

Every day in the rice field the Communist soldiers pushed people to work to their maximum. Whoever didn't have enough energy to work to the maximum had to give up and die on the field. As soon as we finished one field, they moved us to another. We kept moving from place to place, farther and farther away from home. We never lived in one place longer than six months. Our lives were unstable.

The Khmer Rouge separated me from my mom at the beginning of their takeover. As a young kid, nine years old, I missed her. I always dreamed that some day I would be free from this crazy regime. Every night before I went to sleep I always prayed for help. Months passed and I used to think, "I wonder if Mom is still alive, or is she dead?"

One day I decided to run away from my work camp to see my mom. This wasn't an easy thing to do. I had to walk along the road where Communist soldiers were. It was risky. If I got caught, I could be killed. I had an idea. I wrote a fake pass. I walked past the rice field to the corn-field, past one village to another village, past one range of mountains to another. It took me one full day to reach my home. I used my fake pass at the security checkpoints. From the last checkpoint, I could see the roof of my mom's house.

I was so happy that I was about to see my mom. I ran and jumped up and down. When I got close to the yard, I saw that the grass had grown tall, over my head. My heart fell, and my tears dropped like a rainstorm. It was hard to find the path that led to the door of the hut. It looked like people had not walked this way for a long time. I screamed from the yard and ran and opened the front door.

I looked around. I saw no one home. I started calling, "Mom . . . Mom . . . where are you?" I went and asked my neighbors if they knew where my mom was. One elderly person told me that she had been ordered to work in the rice field not too far from home. I knew the place. I went right away to look for her. The sun started setting and darkness had come.

I kept asking people at the field where my mother was. They told me where she was staying. When I got to the place, my mom saw me first but I didn't recognize her. She ran over to me and gave me a big hug. Filled with emotion, we cried for a few minutes, then we started to talk. She had become older than her age. She was weak and skinny. For that joyful moment, we forgot all about our pain.

*HAMSON C. TAING's father died of sickness and one sister died of starvation under the Khmer Rouge. He and his family escaped to Battambang during a Vietnamese attack on the Khmer Rouge. Feeling insecure about the Vietnamese, the family fled Cambodia to Thailand in November 1979. They lived in Thailand until June 1984, when they went to the Philippines. Hamson and his family came to the United States in late October 1984, being sponsored by the International Rescue Committee. Hamson received an associate of science degree in electronics. He lives in Long Beach, California, and works as a contractor. He owns a small sewing shop.*

❀  ❀  ❀

# *The Nightmare*

### HAMSON C. TAING

**W**hat is a nightmare? It is a dream arousing feelings of intense fear, horror, fright, and distress. It happened to me in Mercedes, California, where I slept at my friend Ricky's home. It was in the summer of 1987. As I was sleeping, I heard a truck pass by. Then I felt the Khmer Rouge soldiers chasing me right after they shot my brother-in-law, Suot. Here is what I remembered.

In mid-1978, we were ordered to return from the work farms to the section. My house was located near the river in Section 1, Zone 1, in Battambang province. All people— young and old, men and women—who were split up from their families for several months were forced to rejoin them within twelve hours. My co-workers and I, who were assigned to take care of the sugarcane farm, were very happy to have a reunion with our families. We packed our torn clothes, hammocks, pots, and dishes and went home. We walked, ran, and sang Communist songs merrily along the way.

As I approached home, an old and skinny lady who looked like an alien was sitting in my home doorway, smiling tiredly at me. She wore a torn black blouse and sarong. Her hair was messy. Her skin was wrinkled. I smiled back at her, but I didn't recognize who she was. When I did, I was speechless. I recognized only her soft voice. She said, "Chhay, is it you?" I took a deep breath and stepped up to her with tears running down my cheeks. I held her hands, caressed her arms, and hugged her. It was my mom. We didn't talk except for tears of joy of our reunion.

The bell rang in the distance to let us know that dinner was ready. It was about five at night. Children and adults walked to the worksite, carrying bowls and spoons, ready for dinner. All of the people were very skinny, smelly, and ugly. Some of them looked happy since they were reunited with their families, others looked sad. I only worried about my skinny mother and my siblings because Angka made them work hard and eat less.

Laughing with joy and talking aloud became whispering and a moment of silence as the crowd saw two strangers approach. They wore black uniforms with scarves around their necks, caps on their heads, and AK–47s on their shoulders. A tall, strong, and dark man called Chem was one of them. In 1978 he was to become known as the cruelest and maddest man. He came from eastern Cambodia. He stood up in front of us and his partner went to the back to guard him, forcing us to stay where we were. Mr. Chem beat up and killed men as if they were animals.

He said, "Respectful fathers, mothers, and all friends, I hope you all are very happy to be back here with your families. This evening Angka has sent me here to inform you that Angka has changed work assignments. Angka warns all of you that you are not allowed to go anywhere, especially across the street to the west after dark. If anyone dares to do this, he or she has to take responsibility for him or herself. New assignments will be told to you by tomorrow. Thank you all, and have a nice dinner."

That caused so much anger in my heart. The Khmer Rouge could hold a meeting anywhere or anytime they wanted. And everyone had to pay good attention. No one was allowed to speak up, stand up, or walk away; otherwise, they would be in big trouble. They could be tortured or beaten to death in front of the crowd, as I had heard and seen.

Everyone looked nervous, filled with sorrow. Most of the adults couldn't eat in the worksite. They just carried their bowls of liquid porridge with worry and without saying a word. We noticed that whenever the Khmer Rouge soldiers came they often planned to capture some men, accusing them of doing things against Angka's revolutionary wheel. They tortured and killed them right there or a few miles away. We looked at each other with horror and frustration. Soon after, we went home. We sat around with our family members, whispering about the horrifying event. My oldest brother, Meng, and my brother-in-law Suot had a plan. They would hide and sleep somewhere in the orange farm even though they did nothing wrong because we didn't know when any of us would be taken.

Around seven o'clock, the sound of people yelling and calling names scared us, as if an attack had happened with shells and bombs. I lifted my head and listened to what was going on. Suddenly, a name was called, "Meng's mom, Meng's mom, come and hurry. We need to go now." My mother opened the window and we saw a lady with a full basket on her head. One hand held the basket and the other held her youngest son's hand.

"Hey! Sokha's mom," Mom said.
"Yes," she answered.
"Where are we going?"
"Sister Loum, we need to go to Treng [a jungle near the Thai border] right now! Angka assigned us to go there. No one is allowed to stay here past the next thirty minutes."
"Why?"
"I don't know."

While we were talking, people in the section moved very fast to the west, which was the opposite direction that Mr. Chem told us to go at the worksite. We wondered about the situation as we tried to grasp our pots, dishes, buckets, mats, and as many clothes as we could.

We walked through the darkness. The dirt was blowing in the air. Even though I couldn't see it, I could smell it. We walked about two hours, but no one knew where Treng was. We were very tired. Suddenly an unknown man riding a horse from Treng claimed that the people from Treng were coming our way. We were stuck in the forest. Everyone started to put down their belongings. I laid down against a bush and took a nap. When I woke up, I heard a Khmer Rouge soldier trying to arrest Mao, our section leader, and his guards, who were also Khmer Rouge. We were then accused of betraying Angka. We were scared to go back to the section.

It was about nine–thirty in the morning. The sun rose and it became hot. The people started walking again. That evening we heard that Angka wanted all of us to return home and would pardon everyone who was headed toward Treng. Groups of families split apart. Some didn't trust the Khmer Rouge's propaganda and went on to hide themselves in the deep forest. Others were undecided where to go. My family, consisting of twelve (my mother, three brothers, three sisters, a brother–in–law, sister–in–law, two nieces, and me) went to hide by a grassy lake.

After we found ourselves a spot under a tree near a farm dike by the tall grass, Suot and I tried to go back home to find out what was going on. We didn't walk along the farm dikes because we believed that the Khmer Rouge might see us. Instead, we walked along the mountainside. As we approached our section and were ready to cross the street, I heard a truck coming from the south. By that time Suot was about fifteen meters ahead of me, close to the street. I stopped and hid myself behind a sugarcane bush. My eyes were opened wide, staring toward the oncoming truck. The truck stopped. It was a military truck. It carried Khmer Rouge soldiers.

Some soldiers jumped down and walked toward Suot and said, "Hold on, my comrade." Suot hesitated. Then a few of them pointed guns at him and said, "Hands up."

My heart was beating very fast and my body was shaking and sweating. I almost shouted out loud, telling him to
run, but I couldn't because I was so nervous that I didn't even
realize I had pissed in my pants. Immediately he turned away
from them and ran.

Bang, bang, bang . . . they shot him. I paid no more attention and ran as fast as I could, like a horse, through the
bushes and hills toward the ghostly forest. At this moment
it was the only place I could trust. I thought to myself, "Angka
asked us to come back home and wouldn't punish anyone.
Then why did they shoot Suot?" I believed that he was dead
and that they were still searching for me. Weeping and being
disappointed about the lying Angka propaganda, somehow
I was able to fall asleep.

When I woke up I didn't know where I was or how I had
gotten there. It was dark. My heart was pounding and my
body was trembling. I sat up and decided to get out of those
barbed and bushy trees, but my legs were bleeding and hurt.
My foot was stuck with briars that I had to get out before I
could go on. Even though I had injuries and was tired, I
walked carefully and patiently with a bamboo stick to where
my brother was shot. Arriving there, I kneeled down and
looked closely at the ground around where he had been
standing. I even tried to smell if there was any blood, but I
found nothing. He was gone. Tears started to run down my
cheeks. I sat down for a moment to see if he hid somewhere.
He was nowhere. I felt lonely and full of despair. I decided
to go to the section first before I joined my family.

Approaching home, my name was called, "Chhay, Chhay,"
in a whisper. I stood still and didn't reply. This made me
think of a ghost story that my grandparents and friends used
to tell me. They told me that a ghost could make up any
kind of sounds and knew any name. It made me very scared
and my hair turned up. I thought to myself that this was the
first time I was ever haunted. My eyes opened wider, staring in the direction of the whispering voice. The call went

on, "It's me, Chhay." The voice was coming from the house. "Is it you, brother?" I asked. "Yes, it's me." I felt so relieved. Then I dropped the bamboo stick which I kept in case anyone attacked me.

Suot was safe. He told me that he saw me run too, but he ran in the other direction so the soldiers could chase him alone. He said that after the soldiers chased him for a few minutes, they disappeared. He showed me this magic thing he wore around his waist that protected him. In the dark, we went back to join our family. It was too dark to see, but my family knew that only we could find where they were. They were very worried about us. They asked, "Why are you so late?" We asked them if they had heard any gunshots. They said they had. They said they had heard the Khmer Rouge shoot and kill Phat's wife and children because they planned the escape. But my family wasn't right. It was Suot who the Khmer Rouge shot at. My mother and oldest sister were frightened. They held our hands and thanked God for saving us. Because of the horrifying event, we decided to move on to hide ourselves somewhere in the banana farm by the nearby mountain.

Twenty other families joined us. Along the way I heard that Phat said he would kill all the Khmer Rouge, even the babies in the hammocks, if the country collapsed. We believed that if the Khmer Rouge found us our punishment would be torture or death. We were too tired to care or be scared anymore. What we needed to do was sleep.

When I woke up in the middle of the night my body was blistered and itchy because I slept on poison vines and ants bit me. There was a bigger problem. Because we were so thirsty and it was dark, we couldn't see what was in the water. We didn't care. We drank it. The water not only tasted terrible, but it also had lime in it. About two hours later, I could barely piss. My testicles felt so painful. My urine was full of blood. This also happened to some of the others in our group.

A day later we heard the same news that Angka requested us to go back "home." We had no choice, so we decided it was better to go back home than to be followed. Chem heard what Phat had said earlier about killing all the Khmer Rouge. Later, Chem requested that Phat get some fabric for his family. Three days later Chem told Phat's wife that Phat ran away with three grenades and a pistol he gave to him. Phat was killed with Tuon, an innocent friend who went with him to see Chem. Phat and Tuon's skeletons were found in May 1979 by the hill under the tamarind tree a few miles away from the section. Phat was identified by a blue shirt and Tuon with his black pajama uniform.

Even though seventeen years have gone by, what happened to me seems very fresh because some nights I still have dreams about the violence and punishments that the Khmer Rouge Communist regime used to threaten me, my family, and others between 1975 and 1979. It not only happened in my village and section, but in the whole country. I still don't know why the Khmer Rouge hated us so much. They had no sense of what human beings were at all. They beat up, tortured, and killed people like we were animals, and they enjoyed doing it. They also taught children to hate their parents and said that their parents were Angka's enemies. Some children even killed their own parents. I am very lucky that I wasn't chosen or brave enough to do this.

This regime was terrible. I don't want to see the Khmer Rouge back in power in my lifetime. Now I pray to God to help put mercy in their hearts so that they will realize their wrongful actions. I also pray that our suffering will be healed, starvation will be gone, and peace and justice will come to Cambodia, my beloved homeland.

*SOPHEA MOUTH was twelve when the Khmer Rouge took power. After being separated, his family—except for his mother, who was mortally wounded by the Khmer Rouge—reunited in 1979 amid the crossfire between the Khmer Rouge and Vietnamese soldiers. They escaped to Thailand. At Surin refugee camp it took the family about two months to find sponsorship. On September 12, 1979, they arrived in Lake Geneva, Wisconsin. Sophea is actively involved in local government, working as activist, mediator, and translator. He has a bachelor's degree in political science and an MBA, and he is working toward obtaining a Ph.D. in Buddhist studies with the hopes of becoming a professor.*

❀  ❀  ❀

# Imprinting Compassion

### SOPHEA MOUTH

*If an individual has been exposed to a violent environment, is that individual prone to violence? Can the effect of violence be so strong that it destroys human compassion? A violent environment need only have a short-term effect on human compassion, as it did with me, because compassion cannot be destroyed, it can only be paralyzed temporarily.*

**A** man was holding a sharp ax rotated backward in his right hand, and with his left, he had a firm grip on another man's shoulder. At that instant, the edge of the ax cut open the man's chest. Blood spurted and I heard a roaring groan, loud enough to startle the animals. I stood there smiling deceitfully in shock because it was the first killing I had seen.

After the cadre had opened up the man's chest, he took out the liver. One man exclaimed, "One man's liver is another man's food." Then a second man quickly placed the liver on an old stump where he sliced it horizontally and fried it in a pan with pig grease above the fire that one of the cadres had built.

When the liver was cooked, the cadre leader took out two bottles of rice–distilled whiskey, which they drank cheerfully. I was too young and the cadres didn't allow me to participate in their celebration, although I had no desire to taste human liver.

I considered myself an observer only. One of the cadres had taken me in and had accepted me as a trusted member who could and would be willing to obey commands and share whatever information I could get out of the workers.

As I sat and observed those men using small bamboo stakes to poke the slices of the liver frying in the pan, I thought that they were savages. Their eyes were bloodshot – perhaps they were intoxicated from what they had eaten – and they scowled at me. As soon as they caught me looking at them, they asked me to examine the corpse closely. The odor from the blood was so strong that I threw up.

The cadres exposed me to the killing because they wanted to test my loyalty toward them and Angka. If I showed any reluctance toward seeing their ruthless behavior, they wouldn't have been convinced that I had assimilated into their culture.

This was one of the incidents that touched my heart profoundly. I was paralyzed, unable to move freely knowing that this could happen to me or my relatives. My heart was pounding like a drum.

Though the incident affected me, I had to cope with my life. I did not become a violent person. How much of an effect did the incident have on me? Did it alter my behavior and my compassion entirely? The answer is no, and something that happened to me before the Khmer Rouge came to power, when I was about ten, helped me to remember why.

During the civil war I was sitting below my grandmother's house, which was on stilts. A girl walked straight toward me. She was wearing rags. On her back was a cloth sack sewn together with a white thread. Her complexion appeared to be pale, perhaps from undernourishment, and her cheeks no longer had a glowing look. She was a walking cadaver. After I observed her thoroughly, I was speechless, not because I was disgusted by her appearance, but because she aroused my pity. My initial reaction was to adopt her as a part of my family. I thought that she wouldn't have to go around begging anymore if she was my sister. Even though she was around my age, she addressed me as a superior. "Sir, would you spare me a couple cans of rice?"

I looked her in the eyes. Her eyes suggested that she had been through a great ordeal. They had a look of desperation. I asked her where she was from. She said, "I used to live in Kompong Cham Province and I have been begging for food about nine months. My house was destroyed by the bombing, and the bombs killed my father and two of my brothers. My mother is recovering from injuries to her legs."

Without hesitation I took her cloth sack and went into my house and filled it with about ten pounds' worth of rice. I was very careful not to let anyone in my family know that I had taken some rice and other canned goods and given them to a beggar. I feared that my parents would punish me. Still, I was willing to accept the consequences. I offered to help carry the rice to the place where she was staying because I wanted to find out if what she had said about her family was true.

When she stopped at the edge of the city, I asked where she was staying. She said, "Right here." When I looked in the direction she was pointing, I saw two poles supporting a piece of plastic. Under the plastic was a woman with two amputated legs and a torn blanket covering her body. The mother was curious as to who I was, and the girl explained that I had been very generous to her.

The mother looked at me and said, "Thank you, nephew, for helping me and my daughter. I wish to bless you with all the luck and glory that your fate will not be like mine." I couldn't speak, but tears had reached my cheeks and I wiped them off repeatedly.

Angka's indoctrination was an attempt to destroy all my compassion for another human being. Angka believed that an individual must destroy this "negative" feeling if she or he is to serve the party. At one point I began to accept what Angka had to offer. I accepted their ideas not because my compassion had been destroyed by the indoctrination but because I wanted to live. I was not mad and I was not confused. My mind was clear and I knew what I was doing. I used my wit to deal with the cadres. I was subtle in almost everything I did. I fooled the cadres many times. I had to pretend that Angka was right and that it was justified in whatever it did. Deep inside, though, I knew I could never kill anyone. Angka's indoctrination still causes me to have nightmares.

My feelings for my family help explain my actions. I remembered when the cadre forced my mother to leave her home. She refused, and the cadres shot her right in the neck. She fell to the floor and blood rushed out and there was a puddle of blood on the floor. I was determined not to cry—not that I didn't feel horror, but my heart was frozen.

Later I learned that the cadres had arrested my father. He was a former military leader, and they were going to execute him. He managed to escape during the execution lineup. He came to my aunt's farm to join us, and we lived as farmers for several months. Then Angka decided to purge people with wealthy backgrounds. My father tried hard to conceal his identity. He lied to the cadres that he was a peasant, but the cadres were still suspicious of him.

A peasant woman who didn't like my father claimed to know his identity, and she reported it to Angka. Angka then concocted a scheme to kill my father without alarming the villagers. They reassigned him to a distant zone, but everyone knew that those who were reassigned never returned. It was Angka's usual killing tactic. Fortunately, my father was sick and couldn't go. His life was spared, but he lived in constant fear.

In the midst of the confusion Angka took away my older brother, my oldest sister, my two younger sisters, and my

youngest brother. Angka forced them to dig canals, to transplant rice, and to carry baskets of dirt to build dams. My
older brother said that Angka starved him. Angka gave him
a daily ration of one bowl of rice gruel and he had to sup-
plement his diet by eating raw field crabs or whatever he
could find when the cadres weren't looking. My youngest
brother had to stay in the indoctrination camp. My sisters
were in a similar situation. They became emaciated from
starvation and intensive labor.

Since I lived among peasant farmers, I didn't experience
the kind of pain the others experienced. I mostly observed
pain. I wanted to help those who were not as "fortunate" as
I was by whatever means possible and went out of my way
to help others.

The Pol Pot regime turned some people into fierce human
beings. I know several refugees who used to be killers that
are now leading religious lives. When I asked them why they
did what they did during the Pol Pot regime, they said they
didn't have any choice, and that is why they didn't think
about morality when it came to obeying orders.

For me, I value other people's lives as much as I love my
own. I could not kill anyone because Angka told me to.
Whatever decision I made, it was not to hurt or kill anyone,
but to serve and to protect them whenever I could. Neither
the cadres nor Angka could convert me against my will.
Now, compassion is mine.

RANACHITH "RONNIE" YIMSUT (with family) fled to Thailand in February 1978 after witnessing more than two decades of turmoil and the massacre of nearly his entire family. He became an orphan, prisoner, refugee, immigrant, student, taxpayer, professional, family man, volunteer, and finally an educator and volunteer back in his homeland of Cambodia. Ronnie settled in the United States in late October 1978 from a refugee camp in Thailand. In 1987 he received a bachelor of science degree in landscape architecture, with an emphasis on environmental planning and design, from the University of Oregon. He also specialized in physical and cultural geography, primarily that of Southeast Asia. He has worked as a professional landscape architect and as an environmental planner for the USDA Forest Service since 1987 at two national forests in the Pacific Northwest. He serves as an environmental consultant to the World Monuments Fund, a nonprofit, nongovernmental organization based in New York City, on a ten-year conservation project in Siem Reap Angkor, his birthplace. He is active on issues and concerns facing both the Khmer and American communities. He has returned to Cambodia several times as a volunteer with the Cambodian American National Development Organization (CANDO) and other nongovernmental organizations in an effort to help rebuild his homeland. He has been invited to return to Cambodia for two or three years to work on an environmental conservation product under sponsorship of the United States Agency for International Development, the U.N. Development Program, and other nongovernmental organizations. Ronnie started his own family in 1986 with a Khmer-American wife. They have a daughter and son, and a terrier. Ronnie has contributed his story to the Digital Archive of Cambodian Holocaust Survivors on the Internet.

# The Tonle Sap Lake Massacre

### RONNIE YIMSUT

A pointy object poked at me very hard and woke me up from the muddy bottom of the canal. I slowly opened my eyes to look at a soldier, who continued to poke me with his oversized AK–47 rifle. He was no older than twelve, just a few years younger than I was, but much, much fatter. He was yelling angrily for me to get up from the mud. "Go ahead and shoot me," I said to myself. I was ready to die. It was hopeless. I finally pushed my weak, skinny body up from the mud and wearily walked toward where my group was congregated. It was our time to go, at last. I began to have mixed feelings about the sudden relocation plan. Normally we would stay in one place for weeks or even months at a time before they shipped us out again.

They ordered us to file in rows of four. A small group of soldiers who were to escort us was made up of all ages. Some were as young as ten. There were only five of them to escort what was left of my original group of people. By then there were only seventy–nine of us together. During five awful days at this place, eight of us had died, including six children and two elderly men. I wondered why there were so few of them if they were going to kill all seventy–nine of us.

The oldest soldier came over in front of us and spoke loudly so that everyone could hear him. He told us that we were being moved to Tonle Sap, which meant "Great Lake," to catch fish for the government. He also said that there would be food to eat there. Suddenly people were talking among themselves about the news. We were all very skeptical about this miraculous news, but it made sense, since most of us were once commercial fisherman at Tonle Sap. They told us just what we wanted to hear. The food, the chance to catch and eat fresh fish from the lake and to get away from the misery. It all sounded too good to be true. I was completely fooled by the news. And so were the rest of the people.

They took us south over a familiar muddy road toward Tonle Sap, which was about six or seven miles away. The longer we were on that road the more relaxed we became. Perhaps they were telling us the truth? We seemed to be headed in the right direction. There were only five of them and they can't possibly kill all seventy-nine of us . . . could they?

After about three miles of walking they asked us to stop and wait for the rest of the group. People were very weak, and the three-mile hike took its toll. Another child died on the way. The soldiers allowed the mother to bury her child. It was another twenty or thirty minutes before the rest caught up.

They wanted us to move on quickly with the setting of the sun. They first asked all the able men, both young and old, to come and gather in front of the group. The men were then told to bring all kinds of tools, especially knives and axes, with them. They said the men needed to go ahead of the group to build a camp for the rest of us. The men soon lined up in single file with their tools in hand. I watched my brother, Sarey, as he walked reluctantly to join the line after saying good-bye to his pregnant wife. I told him that I would take good care of Oum, my sister-in-law. The group disappeared shortly as the sky darkened. That was the last time I saw Sarey and the rest of the men again.

The sky was getting darker and it grew chillier. The notorious Tonle Sap mosquitoes began to rule the night sky. After about thirty minutes or so, the two soldiers that had led the men away returned. They quickly conferred with their fellow comrades about something not far away. One or two of the people from my group overheard something quite unbelievable, and the shocking news quickly spread among the people within the group. I learned that they said something like, "a few got away." It only meant one thing: the men were all dead except for a few who managed to escape.

It was about seven or eight o'clock at night when we were ordered to move on again. By this time the children who still had enough energy to cry were crying and screaming as loud as they could. It was mainly from hunger and exhaustion, but also from the attack by the swarming mosquitoes. Above the cry of the children I could hear the sobbing and weeping of the people who had lost their loved ones. The odds were stacked against us. If we didn't die of starvation, exhaustion, or mosquito bites, there was a good chance that we would be killed by the soldiers.

187

The thought of coming face to face with death terrified me for the first time. I thought about escaping right then but after long consideration couldn't do it. I didn't have the heart to leave my family, especially my pregnant sister-in-law, who was already a week overdue. Besides, where would I go from here? I would eventually be recaptured and killed. If I was to die, I preferred to die among my loved ones. There were plenty of opportunities for me to escape, but I just couldn't do it.

I reluctantly trekked with the rest of the group, with my sister-in-law Oum holding onto my right shoulder and a small bag of belongings on my left. It was ironic that night. We knowingly walked toward our death, just like cattle that were being herded to the slaughterhouse. Even the children seemed to know it. But I still had a little hope despite everything I had seen and heard.

A few miles before we were to reach Tonle Sap they ordered

us to turn off to the west instead of continuing down south as planned. It was a very muddy, sticky road. My feet seemed to get stuck in the mud every single time I put them down. Progress was slow and cumbersome. A few people got stuck in the mud, which was just like quicksand, and the soldiers came over to kick and beat them. I never knew if they made it. I was busy helping Oum and myself move forward and didn't really care anymore.

All that time I was trying to calm myself down and keep a clear mind. Oum was beyond help. Her quiet weep had now became a full-blown scream. She was in bad shape physically and emotionally. She said that she had a stomach cramp or was in labor, she wasn't sure. It was to be her first child. She didn't know much about childbirth or contractions, and neither did I. All I could do was to drag her across the muddy flat so that the soldiers wouldn't come and beat us to death. It was pathetic.

We were no more than 300 yards off the main road when they asked us to sit down on the edge of a small shallow canal that ran east to west. Both of our legs were stretched forward, and we had to shut up or they would beat us up. In a matter of minutes a large group of soldiers numbering more than fifty suddenly emerged from a hidden place in the nearby forest. It was really dark by then, but from their silhouettes I could tell that they were soldiers with AK-47 rifles, carbines, and large clubs in their hands. One began to shout loudly to us as the rest surrounded the group, their rifles aimed directly at us. People began to plead for their lives.

The soldiers screamed for all of us to shut up. They said they wished only to ask a few questions. They said they suspected that there were enemies among our group. They claimed there were Vietnamese agents in our group, which was a bogus claim since we had known each other for many years. It was a tactic, their dirty trick to keep us calm, weak, and under control. It was very effective because all the strong men who could have risen against them were the first to go. What was left of the people in my group were women, children, the sick, and the weak. They had us right where they wanted us. It was a premeditated plan.

A soldier walked toward me and yanked a cotton towel from me and shredded it into small strips. I was the first one to be tied up tightly by the soldiers with one of the cotton strips. I was stunned and terrified. I began to resist a little. After a few blows to the head with rifle butts, I let them do as they pleased with me. My head began to bleed from the cuts. I was still semiconscious. I could feel the pain and the blood flowing down my face. They were using me as an example of what one would get if they got any kind of resistance.

They quickly tied the rest of the people without any problems. By this time it was totally chaotic, and people continued to plead for their lives. I was getting more and more dizzy as blood continued to drip across my face and into my right eye. It was the first time that I had tears in my eyes, not from the blood or the pain, but from the reality that was setting in. I became numb with fear.

I was beyond horrified when I heard the clobbering begin. Oum's elderly father was next to me, and his upper torso contracted several times before it fell on me. At that moment I noticed a small boy whom I knew well get up and start to call for his mother. And then there was a warm splash on my face and body. I knew that it was definitely not mud. It was the little boy's blood and perhaps brain tissue that got splattered from the impact.

The rest let out only a short but terrifying sound, and I could hear their breathing stop. Everything seemed to happen in slow motion, and it was so unreal. I closed my eyes but the terrifying sounds continued to penetrate my ear canals and pierce my eardrums. The first blow to hit me came when I was lying face down on the ground. It hit me just below my right shoulder blade. The next one hit me just above the neck on the right side of my head. I heard fifteen more blows, and the victims landed everywhere on my skinny body.

Fortunately, I didn't feel them until much later. I didn't remember anything after that, and I slept very well that night. I woke up to the sound of mosquitoes, which were still buzzing like bees over my body. Only this time there were tons of them feasting on my and the other people's blood. I was unable to move a muscle. My eyes were open, but my sight was blurry. I thought I was blind. I was disoriented. I couldn't remember where I was. I thought I was sleeping at home in my bed. I was wondering why there were so many mosquitoes. Where was I? Why couldn't I move? I was still tied up with the cloth rope. After a few minutes I was able to see a little, but everything else was still blurry. I saw a bare foot in the line of my sight, but I didn't know whose it was.

Suddenly reality set in at full blast and I broke into a heavy sweat. The memories of the event came rushing back and smacked me right in the head. I realized what the sharp dull pain was all over my body and head. I was very cold. I have never been so cold in my entire life. Fear ran rampant in my mind. I suddenly realized where I was and what had happened. Am I already dead? If I am, why do I still suffer like this? I kept asking myself those questions over and over, but could only come to the same conclusion. I am still alive. I am alive! Why? I couldn't understand why I was still alive and suffering. I should have been dead.

The faint light of dawn broke through, revealing my shivering, blood-soaked body in the mud. It must have been about four or five o'clock in the morning on January 1, 1978. "Not a happy New Year today," I thought. It was still dark and cold. My motor skills came back little by little and I was able to move with great difficulty. I pushed myself to sit up by hanging onto the pile of dead bodies. I began to work to untie myself from the cloth rope.

I broke the rope after a few painful tries. My eyesight came back, but after seeing the scattered bodies lying in every direction, I wished that I was blind. Some were beyond recognition. Some were stripped completely naked. Blood-stains that had already turned a dark color gave the area a new dimension. It definitely was not a sight for sore eyes.

I wanted to look for my relatives but was unable to turn around. My neck was stiff with pain. My head hurt, oh, it hurt so bad. I could only feel around me with my hands. Everywhere I touched was cold flesh. My hands were both trembling and I couldn't keep them from shaking. I cried my heart out when I recognized a few dead bodies next to me. One of them was Oum and her unborn child. I suddenly remembered the bare foot I saw when I woke up. It was hers. Her elderly father and two sisters were all part way on top of each other and side by side as though they were embracing just before they lost their lives.

I couldn't go on. My cry turned to a sob, and it was the only sound around besides the mosquitoes, which contin-ued to torment my almost bloodless body. I began to fade and feel as though my life was slipping away. I passed out again on top of the dead bodies.

I woke up to the sound of people coming toward the killing field. I sat up and listened closely. I began to panic. "They are back to finish me off," I told myself. "They are going to bury me alive!" They might as well, I thought. I've nothing to live for. Technically I was already dead. I was ready to give up as the voices were getting closer and louder when my survival instinct finally took control. I pushed myself, inching my way toward nearby bushes. I was no more than twenty feet away from where I was earlier and commanded a good view of the area. The people soon arrived at the site. I was right. They were back with a new batch of victims. Most of the people were men, but a few were women. Their hands were all tightly bounded together with rope.

One of the soldiers gave a command. In broad morning light, I was again witnessing the slaughter of humans. In just seconds they were all clobbered to death just like the rest of my family and friends, whose bodies were still scattered on the muddy ground. My heart just stopped. My entire body shook convulsively and I wanted to throw up. My left hand squeezed tightly over my mouth so that I wouldn't accidentally cry out and give myself away. I felt as though I had gone through the same ordeal all over again. My mind just couldn't take it anymore. I went blank and passed out again.

It was not until the next night that I was really awake. More people were coming toward me again. I assumed that they were more victims to be killed. I didn't wait to find out. I decided then that I wanted to be alive. I began to slip away from the area by crawling on my elbows and knees. I was no longer bleeding, but I knew that I was in bad shape. I was hungry and very thirsty. My lips cracked like mud in the hot sun. I had to find water soon or I would die of thirst. I worked my way west along the shallow dried-up canal and then turned north. By this time it was really dark and chilly again. I found myself in the middle of impenetrable brush and forest. I went back and forth trying to find a way through the thick forest and ended up back where I started, near the killing area.

For the next seventeen days, I hid out in the forest. I slept only at day time, spending my night raiding one village after another for whatever I could find to eat. My injuries healed quickly and I began to put on some weight thanks to the food that I stole from the surrounding villages. I never stayed in one place long. I was on the move and always watching out for any sign of danger. I knew that they were searching for me, and I was able to keep a step or two ahead of them. They always counted bodies, and if one was missing, they searched and usually recaptured the escapees. For seventeen days I was the king of the jungle.

I stumbled accidentally onto a group of escapees who

were also hiding in the forest. I almost got killed because they thought I was a Khmer Rouge spy. The only thing that saved me from certain death was my recent injuries.

We headed for Thailand. After fifteen days of hiking the 150 miles we found ourselves in a Thai jail and then in prison. The Thai authorities considered us political prisoners because we arrived after they closed the border.

Over 600 others like us were kept in a 75–by–75–meter cell. The living conditions were bad and the treatment we got from the Thais was even worse, but I'd rather be in a Thai prison than in the forced labor camps with the Khmer Rouge anytime. At least we were fed and clothed like human beings. Because I was the youngest of the prisoners, I got better treatment. I got to know some of the guards really well, and within four weeks at the Thai border I gained over twenty pounds. I was under eighty pounds when I arrived there.

We all spent five months in the Thai prison before we were moved to a refugee camp near the Thai–Cambodian  border. I waited for a recruitment drive for freedom fighters to fight the Khmer Rouge while I was in the refugee camp, but they didn't accept me because I was "too young and too skinny." I even told them that I was almost eighteen, but it was no use. I couldn't go back to fight, and staying in the camp would only lead me to suicide. I had nothing to live for. I thought that I should end my life just like my fellow refugees who had already killed themselves. But that was too easy! I was a survivor.

My life began to turn around when a CBS news producer named Brian T. Ellis showed up at the camp one day. I was interviewed for a documentary film called *What Happened To Cambodia,* which was later broadcast in the United States. Mr. Ellis took me outside of the camp for the very first time in months. I tasted freedom and I liked it a lot. That day with Mr. Ellis was special and I have never forgotten it. My life began to change for the better after Mr. Ellis left. I now had a reason to go on living. It was a chance for a new life.

I still have nightmares about the massacre on that dark December night. It has never completely gone away from my mind, and I am still horrified just thinking about it. Time does not heal such emotional trauma, at least not for me. I have long since learned to live with it. My life must go on.

# Notes to the Introduction

1. Charles Dickens, *Great Expectations* (London: Penguin 1965), pp. 36–37.

2. The full text of this song is translated in Ben Kiernan, *How Pol Pot Came to Power: A History of Communism in Kampuchea, 1930–1975* (London: Verso, 1985, p. 338.

3. Author's interview, excerpted in David P. Chandler and Ben Kiernan, eds., *Revolution and Its Aftermath in Kampuchea* (New Haven: Yale Council on Southeast Asia Studies, 1983), pp. 182–83.

4. The full text of this song is translated in Ben Kiernan, *The Pol Pot Regime: Race, Power, and Genocide in Cambodia under the Khmer Rouge, 1975–1979*, (New Haven: Yale University Press, 1996), p. 247.

5. Song taught by the Khmer Rouge to children of the Pel family in Battambang in 1978. Author's interview, Toul, 4 November 1979.

6. *Tuol Sleng Personnel Files*, copies held by Cambodian Genocide Program, Yale University, folder 1, document 1, pp. 5–10. Information on the applicant's friends was sought in the final five questions on p. 11 of the same form.

7. *Tuol Sleng Personnel Files*, folder 1, document 1, pp. 6–8.

8. For a full account of the two boys' stories, see Ben Kiernan and Chanthou Boua, *Peasants and Politics in Kampuchea, 1942–1981*, (London: Zed Books, 1982), pp. 334–338.

9. Dickens, *Great Expectations*, p. 73.

# Glossary

**Angka:** The politburo of the Khmer Rouge. The word stems from the great Cambodian empire that ruled Cambodia until the twelfth century. The largest temple complex in the world, Angkor Wat, was built during the empire.

**Buddhism:** The state religion of the Cambodian people. Buddhism is founded on the principles of nonviolence and creating good karma in life by making a conscious effort to do good and become a better person, especially inwardly.

**Freedom Fighters:** A Cambodian group of guerrilla fighters who fought with the Vietnamese to defeat the Khmer Rouge in January 1979. This group led many Cambodians safely across the border into the Thai refugee camps.

**Khmer Republic:** The government of Lon Nol, which ruled Cambodia from March 1970 to April 17, 1975. This pro-West government, which ousted Prince Sihanouk, was defeated by the Khmer Rouge.

**Khmer Rouge:** The "Red Khmers" made up the Cambodian Communist Party, which became powerful during the Vietnam War. After five years of civil war, the Khmer Rouge, led by Pol Pot, overthrew Lon Nol's Khmer Republic on April 17, 1975. The Khmer Rouge attempting to turn Cambodia into an agrarian society, forced all Cambodians into the countryside to work in forced labor camps. They abolished all institutions, the family, and religion. During their reign it is estimated that 2 million Cambodians were murdered, starved, and killed by disease. No one was spared, including children, the elderly, the disabled, the religious, and the minorities. The Khmer Rouge ruled until January 7, 1979, when the Vietnamese invaded and installed a reformed Cambodian Communist government called the People's Republic of Kampuchea.

# GLOSSARY

**Krama:** A traditional Cambodian scarf worn around the neck, head, or body.

**Lon Nol:** A pro-West military leader who overthrew Prince Sihanouk and the monarchy in March 1970. A patriot, Lon Nol opposed Sihanouk's policies of allowing the Communist Vietnamese and the Khmer Rouge to become a strong force inside Cambodia. He transformed Cambodia into the Khmer Republic, which was allied with the West. He fled Cambodia two weeks before the Khmer Rouge took power.

**Mobile youth groups:** During the Khmer Rouge reign, children were separated into work groups according to age and sex. These groups were often sent far from the forced labor camps for extended periods of time to work on such projects as cutting timber and building dams.

**New people (or city people):** People who lived in the cities during the civil war in Cambodia. The cities were controlled by Lon Nol and his army until the fall of Phnom Penh to the Khmer Rouge. The Khmer Rouge despised this group because they thought that city people were corrupted by the "imperialistic" ways of America.

**Old people (or village people):** People who lived in Khmer Rouge "liberated" zones during the civil war with Lon Nol. The Khmer Rouge trusted these people more than city people and gave them better treatment.

**People's Republic of Kampuchea:** On January 7, 1979, the Vietnamese liberated the Cambodian people from the Khmer Rouge. The Vietnamese installed a Cambodian government led by Hun Sen. This government ruled Cambodia until democratic elections took place in 1993. A coalition government currently holds power in Cambodia; it includes Prince Ranariddh (the son of Prince Sihanouk) who is the head of the National United Front for an Independent, Neutral, Peaceful and Cooperative Cambodia, and members of the former People's Republic of Kampuchea, including Hun Sen.

**Phnom Penh:** The capital of Cambodia.

**Pol Pot:** Born Saloth Sar, Pol Pot was educated in France, where Communist ideas were popular among French students. He changed his name in the 1950s to Pol Pot when he joined the underground Communist party in the jungles of Cambodia. The Khmer Rouge under his leadership came to power on April 17, 1975, and reigned until they were overthrown by the Vietnamese army on January 7, 1979. Pol Pot and his party are responsible for the deaths of approximately 2 million Cambodians during his reign of terror, called the killing fields.

**Reeducate:** A term used by the Khmer Rouge. It meant to brainwash or execute. In the forced labor camps the Khmer Rouge wanted everyone to forget the old Cambodian society, and they sent people to long meetings to be brainwashed. Some were taken away to be killed.

**Prince Norodom Sihanouk:** As prince, Sihanouk ruled Cambodia from 1955 until he was deposed by Lon Nol in 1970. Swaying from his original policy of neutrality during the late 1960s, Sihanouk allied with Communist Vietnam and allowed it to use land along the Cambodia-Vietnam border as a military sanctuary and supply route. When Sihanouk lost power in 1970, he went to China where he became nominal president of the Khmer Rouge. He maintained this status until 1976 when the Khmer Rouge then held him under house arrest. Freed in 1978, he fled to China where he currently maintains his residence.